Science

Steven Goldsmith
Senior Advisor (Secondary and Assessment)
Stockton-on-Tees

ISBN: 0 563 47433 5

Published by BBC Educational Publishing
First published 1999
Reprinted in 2000
2nd reprint May 2000

Designed by Cathy May (Endangered Species)
Illustrated by Kathy Baxendale
Reproduced and printed in Great Britain by sterling

Contents

Bitesize Key Stage 3 Science

Introduction   4

Biology

Life processes and cell activities   7

Humans as organisms 1   11
Digestion, movement and respiration

Humans as organisms 2   16
Circulation, reproduction and health

Green plants as organisms   20

Variation and classification   24

Living things in their environment   28

Chemistry

Classifying materials   32

Changing materials   38

Chemical reactions   42

Metals and non-metals   46

Acids and alkalis   50

Physics

📺 🔊 Electricity and magnetism   53

📺 🔊 Forces and motion   57

📺 🔊 Light and sound   62

📺 🔊 The Earth and beyond   67

📺 Energy resources and transfer   70

Answers to practice questions   *73*

Index   *77*

Introduction

About Key Stage 3 Bitesize Revision

Key Stage 3 Bitesize Revision will help you do your best in the Key Stage 3 National Tests. It comprises:

> KS3 Bitesize Science: this book!
> ISBN: 0 563 47433 5

> The KS3 Bitesize Science CD-ROM
> ISBN: 0 563 47467 X
> provides step-by-step explanations and extra practice material

> TV programmes
> (also available on video)
> ISBN: 0 563 47436 X
> 0 563 47444 0

> The website:
> www.bbc.co.uk/revision
> to get more practice in those areas that you find difficult

This science book will help those of you hoping to achieve Levels 5, 6 and 7 in the tests. Don't forget to use your notes from school and any textbooks you have been using as well.

Each of the 16 sections in the book covers science topics that you will have been taught during Key Stage 3 (Years 7, 8 and 9).

- Each section begins with a number of introductory pages that summarise the main ideas in the section.

- Next is the FactZONE, which has the key facts, definitions of important ideas, diagrams and equations that you need to learn.

- Lastly, there is an example of an actual test question. The answers to these questions and advice about how you should answer each part to get the most marks possible are given at the back of the book.

The TV programmes and website have cross-references to show where the book has more information. The book has TV and website symbols (see next page) to show you where there is more information.

Using the TV programmes and website

The programmes are broadcast in the middle of the night, so you will have to record them on video. Remember to set the video the night before! Key Stage 3 BITESIZE videos are also available to buy. Using them on video means you can go back over the bits you are not sure of as many times as you like.

Have this BITESIZE Science book with you as you watch the videos. Do not try to watch a whole tape at once – watch one BITE and then work through that section in the book.

Key Stage 3 Science

The National Curriculum programme of study for Key Stage 3 science is divided into four Attainment Targets: These are:

Sc 1   Experimental and investigative science
       (this will probably be called Scientific Enquiry after 2000)

Sc 2   Life processes and living things

Sc 3   Materials and their properties

Sc 4   Physical processes.

The science tests

The Key Stage 3 tests in science that you take near the end of Year 9 contain questions that cover Sc 2, Sc 3 and Sc 4. There are an equal number of marks available in each of these three parts. Your teacher will assess your attainment in Sc 1 from the work you do during the course. Everybody has to take the tests. There are two test papers and each test lasts one hour.

Using this book to revise

- Plan your revision carefully. You'll take your Key Stage 3 science tests in early May. It's a good idea to start your revision at least two months before you take your tests to be sure you have enough time to cover all of the sections in this book. It's no good leaving your revision until the last moment.

- Break the subject up into BITESIZE chunks. That is why this book is divided into small sections. There are 16 in this book – you need to decide how many you must cover each week to get it all done before your tests. You could use the Contents page to plan your revision timetable. On your timetable, record your plan by writing the date when you plan to work on each section alongside it.

- Plan the revision of all your test subjects at the same time. Make sure you have breaks and time to relax; and organise your revision around sports, hobbies and your favourite TV programmes!

KEY TO SYMBOLS

📺 A link to the video

🌐 On-line service

You can find extra support, tips and answers to your exam queries on the BITESIZE internet site. The address is http://www.bbc.co.uk/revision

Revision tips

You revise best when you are actively doing something.

- Write down the important words and ideas as you work through each section.

- At the end of each section close the book and write down the key facts and ideas.

- For a labelled diagram, copy the diagram then close the book and add the labels.

- For particular spellings and equations, 'Look, cover, write' and then 'check'.

- Write a set of summary notes for each section and rewrite them, in full, first copying the originals and then from memory.

- Test yourself by writing a key word on one side of a piece of card and the definition or explanation on the other.

- Revise with a friend – use the cards to test each other.

- Record your notes onto an audio tape and make notes as you listen to yourself reading.

- Make a set of revision cards that fit into your pocket – test yourself on your way to school!

In the test: make sure you gain the marks!

The markers can only judge how good your answer is by what you write on the paper.

- Read the question carefully before you start to answer.

- Make sure you follow all of the instructions in the question.

- When you have to choose a word from a list, use only the words provided.

- Write your answer clearly and precisely.

- If you make a mistake, ensure that your first answer is crossed out and that it is clear which answer you want the marker to read.

- Show the steps in your calculations as well as the answer.

- Draw or add to diagrams using a pencil and ruler.

- Do not tick any more boxes than you are asked to in the question.

With careful, planned revision you will answer the test questions confidently and gain all of the marks you deserve!

Life processes and cell activities

This section is about

- the organs that enable life processes to take place in plants and animals

- the functions of the parts of plant and animal cells

- the differences between plant and animal cells

- how some cells are adapted to their functions

Living things (or organisms) are alive because of the processes that go on inside them. Each of these life processes plays a part in making sure that the organism stays alive. Most organisms have organs. The organs have a special structure to enable them to perform a particular function. The tables below show some examples of life processes in animals and plants.

Animals

Life process	Organ	Function
movement	muscle	exerts forces on the skeleton
sensitivity	eye	collects information from the environment
excretion	kidney	removes waste from the blood

Plants

Life process	Organ	Function
growth	leaf	site of photosynthesis
reproduction	ovary	produces egg cells
nutrition	root hair	absorbs water and dissolved minerals

Some organisms are large and complex, with a number of different organs. This allows them to carry out a range of activities. Other organisms are simpler, with just enough organs to make sure their life processes take place.

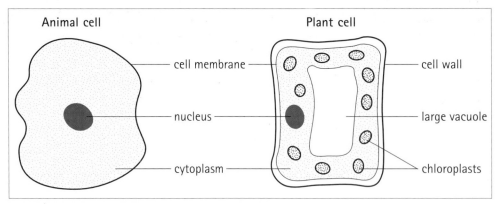

Parts of an animal cell and a plant cell

◉ Cells

All organisms are made up of cells. These are the smallest units of all living things. All cells have a nucleus, cytoplasm and a cell membrane (see diagrams above). Plant cells also have a cell wall, a large vacuole and chloroplasts.

- The wall of the plant cell is on the outside of the cell membrane. It is made from cellulose and it provides support to the cell, helping it to keep its shape.

- The large vacuole contains a solution of sugars and salts called cell sap. The vacuole is close to the centre of the cell and takes up most of the cell's volume.

- The chloroplasts contain the green pigment chlorophyll, which traps light for use in photosynthesis – the process by which plants make their food.

Specialised cells

There are different sorts of cells in both plants and animals. These different cells carry out different functions and are suited in particular ways to those functions. Although the cells shown below share some common features, they look very different. The structure of each cell is one of the ways in which it is adapted to perform its function.

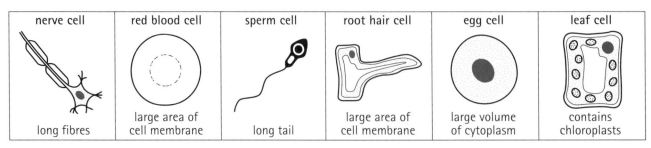

Some specialised cells

FactZONE

⊡ ◎ Life processes

There are seven life processes common to all plants and animals:

Movement

Animals can move from place to place to find food and safety. Plants move slowly by growing in particular directions.

Reproduction

All living things can produce offspring to replace individuals who die.

Sensitivity

All living things can detect changes both inside and outside them. They can respond to most of these in order to survive.

Growth

The permanent increase in size that may take place throughout life but particularly when a living thing is young.

Respiration

The release of energy from food for use within a living thing.

Excretion

The removal of the waste products of chemical reactions that take place inside a living thing.

Nutrition

The process by which living things obtain nutrients. These provide a source of energy, the raw materials for growth and the substances needed to stay healthy.

A simple way to remember this list is that the name MRS GREN has the first letters of the seven life processes given on the left.

⊡ ◎ Cells

All living things are made up of cells. Cells make up the tissues and organs of all organisms. The cells of both plants and animals contain the following parts:

Cell membrane

This is the outer surface of the cell. It controls what passes into and out of the cell.

Nucleus

This controls the chemical activity of the cell and contains the genetic material.

Cytoplasm

This is the watery, jelly-like liquid that fills the cell. It contains the other parts of the cell and is where important chemical reactions take place.

Parts present in BOTH plant and animal cells	Parts present ONLY in plant cells
Cell membrane	Cell wall
Nucleus	Large vacuole
Cytoplasm	Chloroplasts

Practice question – Life processes and cell activities

The diagram below shows a cell from the inside of a human cheek.

a) Label the parts A, B and C. *3 marks*

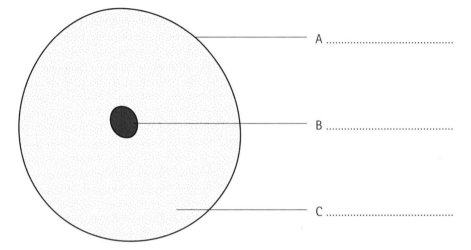

A ....

B ....

C ....

b) Plant cells have some parts that animal cells do **not** have.

Name **two** of these parts. *2 marks*

Humans as organisms 1

This section is about

- a balanced diet, the components of a balanced diet and some sources of those components

- the process of digestion

- the role of the skeleton, joints and muscles in movement

- lung structure and how gas exchange takes place

- the process of respiration

⊚ Food and digestion

The things that humans need for a complete diet are carbohydrates, fats, fibre, minerals, proteins, vitamins and water. A balanced diet is essential for good health.

The amount of these things that you need depends on your age, occupation and leisure activities. A young child, an athletic teenager and a pregnant mother all need the same things but in different quantities. Few foods contain all of these things, which is why it is important to eat a variety of foods.

Component	Used in the body to	Food source
carbohydrates	provide energy	bread, potatoes
fats	store energy	butter, oil
fibre	help food to pass through the body	vegetables, wholemeal bread
minerals	make and maintain specialist cells	spinach, milk, salt
proteins	grow and repair the body	meat, fish, cheese
vitamins	control chemical processes	dairy products, fruit, vegetables
water	dissolve food so that it can move through the body	fruit juice, milk, vegetables

The two most important things that food provides are:

- energy   released from carbohydrates during respiration. This is essential to keep your body working

- chemicals   (mainly proteins) needed for growth and also to repair your body.

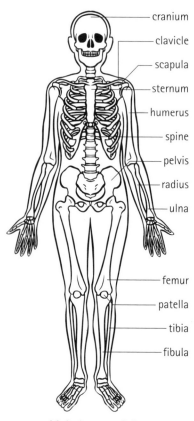

food enters gut

food molecules getting smaller

digested food absorbed into the bloodstream

undigested food egested

How food is processed by the body

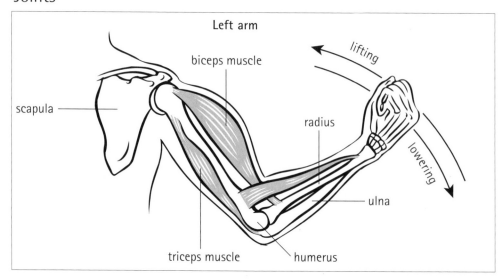

cranium
clavicle
scapula
sternum
humerus
spine
pelvis
radius
ulna
femur
patella
tibia
fibula

Main bones of the skeleton

📺 🖉 Digestion

You must digest your food before you can use it in your body. Digestion is the process by which large molecules of food are made smaller until your body can absorb them.

Digestion starts as soon as you put food into your mouth and it makes food small enough to swallow (see diagram on left). At various points in your digestive system substances called enzymes become involved. These chemicals are biological catalysts. They increase the speed at which the chemical reactions of digestion take place.

Products of digestion

Your blood absorbs the small soluble molecules produced during digestion when they reach the small intestine. The blood system carries them around the body to the cells where they are needed. Some of the molecules in your food do not dissolve and are not digested. These waste materials pass through your body and are removed as faeces. This process is called egestion.

📺 🖉 The skeleton and movement

The skeleton (see diagram on left) is the system of bones and soft tissues, ligaments, muscles and tendons that are linked together.

The human skeleton:

■ supports the body

■ protects vital organs

■ allows the body to move.

Joints

Left arm

lifting

biceps muscle

scapula

radius

lowering

ulna

triceps muscle

humerus

The biceps and triceps: an antagonistic pair of muscles

There are several structures and tissues that are important in allowing the body to move. Joints are points in the skeleton where two bones meet. The table below gives the names and examples of the three types of joint.

Type of joint	Example
immovable	between bones of skull
slightly movable	between vertebrae of the spine
freely movable	between humerus and scapula (see diagram page 12)

Ligaments, muscles and tendons

Ligaments are the tough, fibrous and slightly stretchy tissues that hold the bones together at each joint. They prevent the joint from dislocating.

Muscles are the strong, stretchy tissues that can contract to pull two bones together. They cannot push bones apart. This has to be done by another muscle pulling the bones in the opposite direction as the first muscle relaxes. The pair of muscles moving the bones in opposite directions on either side of a joint is called an antagonistic pair of muscles. An example of an antagonistic muscle pair is shown at the bottom of page 12.

Tendons are strong non-stretchy tissues that attach muscles to bones. If tendons are damaged then the muscles to which they are attached will not work properly and moving that part of the body will become difficult and possibly painful.

ⓣⓥ ◉ Respiration

In order to obtain energy from food, you need a supply of oxygen for the process of aerobic respiration to take place. This oxygen is obtained from the air that you breathe through your mouth and nose.

The air passes down the trachea (windpipe), which divides into two tubes called bronchi, each connected to one of the two lungs. Inside each lung the bronchus divides into many narrower tubes called bronchioles, and at the end of each bronchiole is an air sac. These air sacs are called alveoli.

Gas exchange

The alveoli have a very large surface area, which is very thin, moist and has a good supply of blood vessels. This is where gas exchange happens. Oxygen from the air dissolves in the surface moisture and passes into the blood stream. At the same time, carbon dioxide in the blood passes out through the moist surface into the alveoli. The air then passes back along the same route and is breathed out through the mouth and nose.

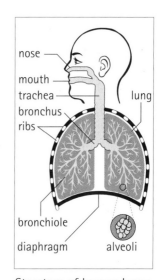

Structure of human lungs

Oxygen transport

The oxygen is carried around the body in the blood system. Once it reaches the cells where it is needed it can react with the food molecules produced by digestion to release energy. This process is called aerobic respiration. Glucose (a carbohydrate) reacts with oxygen to release energy, with the production of carbon dioxide and water. This reaction can be summarised in a word equation:

$$\text{glucose} + \text{oxygen} \xrightarrow{\text{energy released}} \text{carbon dioxide} + \text{water}$$

Some words you should know

Enzymes

molecules that speed up chemical reactions that take place in the body

Egestion

the process of passing undigested waste products out of the body

Tissue

a group of cells with a similar function, which join together to form an organ

System

a group of organs that work together to carry out several related functions

Respiration

the process by which the cells of living organisms release energy by breaking down complex molecules into simpler ones

Aerobic respiration

respiration that takes place using oxygen

Key ideas

- Digestion is the process of making food soluble and useable by the body.

- The bones of the skeleton and the soft tissues work together to allow the body to move.

- Muscles work in pairs. They contract and pull on bones. They relax when other muscles pull the bones in the opposite direction.

- Aerobic respiration can be summarised by the word equation:

$$\text{glucose} + \text{oxygen} \xrightarrow{\text{energy released}} \text{carbon dioxide} + \text{water}$$

Practice question – Humans as organisms 1

Drawings A, B, C, D and E show the positions of the five organ systems in the human body.

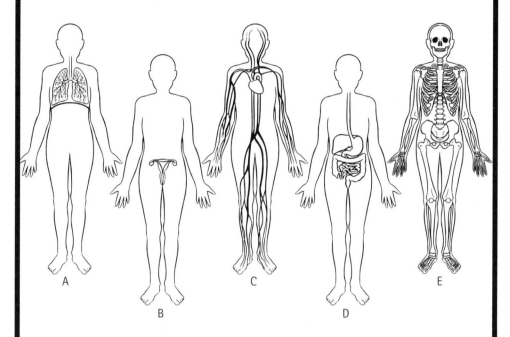

A   B   C   D   E

a) The table below lists the five organ systems. Write the letter of one of the drawings next to the name of the organ system that matches it.

5 marks

Name of organ system	Letter of the drawing of the organ system
circulatory system	
digestive system	
reproductive system	
respiratory system	
skeleton	

b) Which one of the organ systems above is completely different in a man and a woman?

1 mark

Humans as organisms 2

This section is about

- the function of the blood

- the human reproductive system

- the processes involved in human reproduction

- how smoking and the abuse of other drugs affect health

- the causes of disease and ways to maintain and improve health

Boys
bodies become more muscular
voice breaks
hair grows on face, chest and armpits
pubic hair grows
penis becomes larger
sperm begins to be produced

Girls
hips widen
hair grows in armpits
pubic hair grows
breasts develop
eggs begin to be released and periods begin

Secondary sexual characteristics

📺 🔲 The blood system

Blood transports substances to and from the cells of the body. It carries digested food, oxygen and hormones to the parts of the body that need them. It carries away waste products and carbon dioxide. These substances enter and leave the blood through thin-walled blood vessels called capillaries.

📺 🔲 The reproductive system

Reproduction in humans is a sexual process. This means that specialised cells called gametes are needed from a male and a female to produce a new individual. The male gamete is the sperm and the female gamete is the egg.

Puberty and adolescence

The testes of boys start to produce sperm between the ages of 12 and 16. The ovaries of girls start to release eggs between the ages of 11 and 15. This period is called puberty. During adolescence, which follows puberty, there are many other changes to the bodies of both boys and girls. These secondary sexual characteristics are summarised in the table on the left.

As well as these physical changes, boys and girls experience emotional changes, such as insecurity, greater independence and a greater interest in the opposite sex. All of these changes are caused by hormones that are released into the blood.

Eggs develop in the ovaries of a woman. Each month an egg is released from one of the ovaries. This is called ovulation. When ovulation occurs the lining of the uterus becomes thicker, with a greater supply of blood. If the egg does

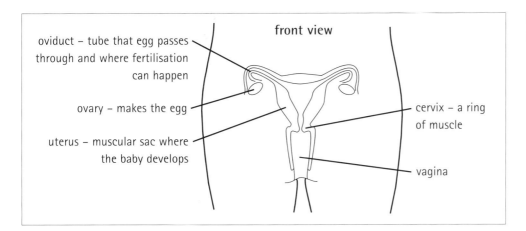

Female reproductive system

oviduct – tube that egg passes through and where fertilisation can happen

ovary – makes the egg

uterus – muscular sac where the baby develops

front view

cervix – a ring of muscle

vagina

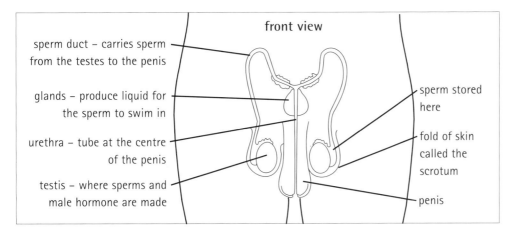

Male reproductive system

sperm duct – carries sperm from the testes to the penis

glands – produce liquid for the sperm to swim in

urethra – tube at the centre of the penis

testis – where sperms and male hormone are made

front view

sperm stored here

fold of skin called the scrotum

penis

not meet a sperm, it breaks down, together with the lining of the uterus, and they pass out of the vagina during the woman's monthly bleeding period. These events, which take place about once every 28 days, make up the menstrual cycle.

Fertilisation

If sperm are released from the penis during sexual intercourse, they swim into the uterus and travel towards the ovary, along the oviduct. There they may meet an egg. If the nucleus of a sperm cell successfully joins with the nucleus of an egg then fertilisation has taken place. A new individual has started to develop and the woman is now pregnant. The fertilised egg begins to divide into a ball of cells called an embryo, which attaches itself to the lining of the uterus and grows as the cells continue to divide.

Development and birth

After 7–8 weeks the organs of the body begin to develop and the foetus, as it is now called, is attached to the placenta by the umbilical cord. In the placenta the blood vessels of the foetus are close to those of the mother. Food and oxygen pass from the mother's blood into that of the foetus. Carbon dioxide and other waste products pass from the blood supply of the foetus to that of the mother. These substances move to and from the foetus along the umbilical cord. After about nine months of development inside its mother's womb the baby is born through the vagina.

⊞ ◉ Smoking and health

❗ R E M E M B E R Pregnant women who smoke have tar and nicotine in their blood, which is passed to the fetus. They also have less oxygen in their blood. On average, women who smoke during pregnancy give birth to smaller, less healthy babies than women who don't smoke.

Smoking has these long-term affects on health:

■ smoke damages the alveoli in the lungs, making it harder to breathe

■ tar from the burning tobacco is deposited in the lungs, where chemicals in the tar can cause lung cancer

■ nicotine from the burning tobacco can cause high blood pressure, which damages arteries

■ carbon monoxide in tobacco smoke reduces the amount of oxygen carried by the blood.

⊞ ◉ Drugs and health

All drugs, including those in cigarette smoke, affect the ways in which the brain and the nervous system work. Many drugs are medicines that, when they are used properly, prevent or treat disease. Any drug that is misused can cause physical damage to the body as well as personal and social problems. For example, large quantities of alcohol will slow down the action of the drinker's brain, making them clumsy, slow to react and have difficulty in making decisions. Continued abuse of alcohol over a long period will result in damage to the liver and the brain. Drugs such as heroin and cocaine can have particularly rapid affects on health, with large doses often causing death.

⊞ ◉ Microbes and disease

❗ R E M E M B E R Bacteria and viruses are microbes that cause many infectious diseases. Bacteria cause cholera, typhoid, tuberculosis and syphilis. Viruses cause influenza, polio, German measles and AIDS.

Organisms that cause disease are called pathogens. The human body has a range of natural defences against pathogens, but sometimes the body needs help to resist the effects of the pathogens and to destroy the poisonous substance that they produce in the body. This can be done in two ways:

■ medicines can be taken to attack the bacteria that cause the disease. Unfortunately, these medicines, called antibiotics, do not affect viruses

■ vaccines can be given to encourage the body's natural defence system to produce antibodies, which are molecules that resist and destroy the cause of the infection. This process is called immunisation.

FactZONE

Some words you should know

Hormone

a chemical that produces a specific change in an organism

Gamete

the reproductive cell of an organism, which can be either male or female

Adolescence

the period of development between puberty and sexual maturity

Testes

the organs in males where sperm cells are produced

Fertilisation

the joining together of a male and female gamete

Key ideas

- Blood is the transport system that carries both useful substances and waste products around the body.

- Sexual reproduction requires the fusion of gametes from two parents.

- In most women the menstrual cycle takes about 28 days.

- Fertilisation takes place when a sperm successfully fuses with an egg.

- The placenta has a vital function in the development of a foetus within the uterus.

- The development of a foetus is at risk if the mother smokes during pregnancy.

- Smoking and the misuse of other drugs have long-term effects on health.

- Medicines and immunisation can increase the body's natural defences against the effects of pathogens.

Practice question – Humans as organisms 2

a) Choose words from the list to complete the following three sentences about the menstrual cycle.

a daily   the uterus
the middle   an ovary
a weekly   the beginning
a monthly   the end
the vagina

Menstruation is part of _____ cycle.

The cycle begins when the lining of _____ breaks away.

An ovum (egg) is released from _____ at about _____ of each cycle.

4 marks

b) During adolescence, boys' bodies change. Describe TWO of the changes.

2 marks

Green plants as organisms

This section is about

- the process of photosynthesis

- the nutrients that are required for plant growth

- the main parts of a plant and their functions

- sexual reproduction in flowering plants

- how plants respire to release energy for life processes

📺 ◉ Photosynthesis

Photosynthesis is the chemical reaction by which plants produce new cell material. Glucose (a type of sugar) is the main product of the reaction and oxygen is a waste product. The glucose is used by the plant to make other compounds that it uses to grow. The plant releases most of the oxygen into the atmosphere and other living things use it in aerobic respiration.

Carbon dioxide and water are chemically combined in photosynthesis and light is needed to provide the energy for the reaction. The light is captured by the green pigment called chlorophyll, which is stored inside structures called chloroplasts. Only cells with chloroplasts can photosynthesise. Without light the cell does not have enough energy for photosynthesis to take place. Photosynthesis can be summarised in this word equation:

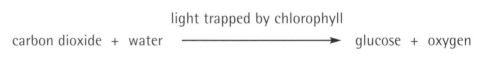

carbon dioxide + water $\xrightarrow{\text{light trapped by chlorophyll}}$ glucose + oxygen

Essentials for healthy growth

Plants also need other elements for healthy growth. Plant roots absorb nitrogen from the soil mainly as nitrates dissolved in water. Iron and magnesium are obtained in the same way. When plants lack these minerals it restricts their growth; they are more likely to become diseased and the quantity and quality of the fruit they produce is reduced. Farmers and gardeners often add fertilisers to the soil to avoid these problems.

In order to absorb water and dissolved minerals, the roots of a plant have special cells called root hair cells at their surface. They have long, hair-like shapes extending out from the cell (see diagram left). These provide a large surface area for absorbing water and dissolved mineral salts from the soil.

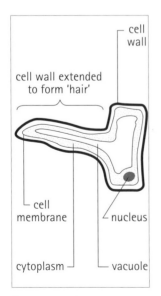

Structure of a root hair cell

📺 🔊 Sexual reproduction

Flowering plants are able to reproduce themselves. The flowers contain the structures that enable sexual reproduction to take place.

Flowers are made up of:

sepals   on the outside of the flower to protect it

petals   inside sepals and often coloured to attract pollinating animals

stamens   the male sex organs. They consist of an anther at the end of a long filament. The anthers produce pollen, which contains the male gamete

carpels   the female sex organs. They consist of three parts – the style, stigma and ovary; the style connects the stigma to the ovary. The ovary produces the ovules, which contain the female gametes.

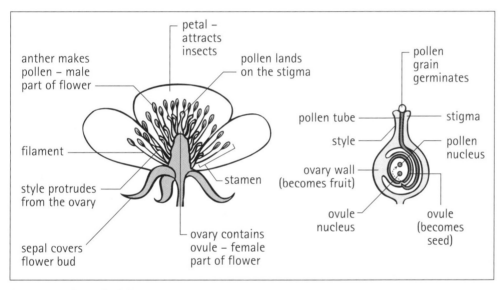

Structure of a typical flower

Pollination

The transfer of pollen from a stamen to a carpel is called pollination. Different flowers are adapted in different ways to make this happen. Some are adapted to receive pollen carried by the wind, some are adapted to receive pollen carried by insects and others are adapted to receive pollen carried by birds and animals.

Fertilisation and seed dispersal

Fertilisation takes place in the ovary and occurs when the male gamete from the pollen fuses with the female gamete in the ovule. The fertilised ovule forms a seed inside the ovary, which itself develops into a fruit.

The fruits of different flowers are adapted in a variety of ways to ensure that the plant's seeds are dispersed away from the parent:

- some will burst open, scattering the seeds over a wide area
- some will be carried in the wind
- some will be eaten or carried away by animals and dropped well away from the parent plant.

Seeds that are successfully dispersed away from the parent plants are more likely to germinate and produce new plants.

! REMEMBER In photosynthesis, carbon dioxide and water react together using light energy to produce glucose and oxygen.

Respiration in plants

Some of the oxygen that plants produce during photosynthesis is used to release energy from sugar by respiration. Plants need this energy to:

- grow
- take up minerals from the soil
- move
- make specialised cells.

Respiration involving oxygen is called aerobic respiration, which can be summarised in this word equation:

$$glucose + oxygen \xrightarrow{\text{energy released}} carbon\ dioxide + water$$

Some words you should know

Gamete

reproductive cell with half of the genetic information of a cell from the body of the organism. It is capable of joining with a gamete of the other sex, from which offspring develop

Fruit

the fleshy swollen ovary, containing the mature seeds

Key ideas

- Photosynthesis is a vital chemical process that requires the presence of light. It takes place in the green parts of a plant.
- Flowering plants are able to reproduce themselves by a process of sexual reproduction.
- Aerobic respiration is the process by which plants produce the energy they need for their life processes.

Practice question – Green plants as organisms

a) The diagram below shows a section through a flower from a cherry tree.

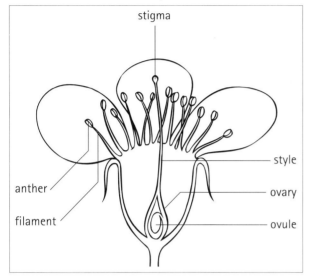

i) Which part becomes the seed? *1 mark*

ii) Which part becomes the fruit? *1 mark*

iii) What is the function of the anther?

1 mark

b) The drawings below show the fruits of two different plants.

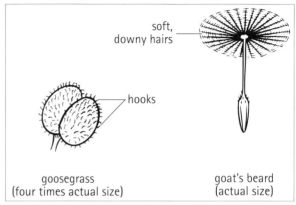

goosegrass
(four times actual size)

goat's beard
(actual size)

For **each** fruit, suggest how its structure helps the seeds to be scattered away from the parent plant.   *2 marks*

c) Explain why it is an advantage to plants that their seeds are scattered far apart.

1 mark

Variation and classification

This section is about

- variation between and within species

- environmental and inherited causes of variation

- the general features of selective breeding

- the five major groups of living things

- the features of the major groups in the animal kingdom

Some human variation!

☎ ◉ What is variation?

All living things can be sorted into groups. The members of each group have similar features. The process of sorting living things into groups is called classification. A group of living things that have many similar features and that can successfully interbreed is called a species. Different species have different features. For example, cats are one species and dogs are another.

There will be differences between individuals within a species. This is called variation. For example, human beings have two legs, a skeleton and a nose between two eyes, but we do not all have the same eye colour, facial features or body shape (see diagram on left). The causes of variation between members of the same species can be either inherited or environmental.

Inherited causes of variation

Offspring look more or less like one or both of their parents. Human children inherit certain characteristics from their parents, such as eye colour, hair colour, nose and ear shape. The 'plans' for these inherited features are carried inside the nucleus of every cell on chromosomes. The offspring of any living thing inherits this genetic information from one or more of their parents. In most animals this can make every individual different from every other individual. In some plants this can make all of the offspring exactly the same as the parent plant.

Environmental causes of variation

The information that offspring inherits from its parents is not the only thing that decides the characteristics of an individual. The conditions in which the offspring grow up will also have an effect. If a human child has two tall

> **❗ REMEMBER**
> Anything in the environment that can affect an individual as it grows and develops can cause variation between that individual and others of the same species.

parents and inherits the potential to be tall, they could still turn out to be quite short if they do not eat a balanced diet.

More generally, the way the child is brought up, what he/she eats, the education he/she receives and the amount of exercise he/she takes can all have an effect on the appearance and characteristics of that child when fully grown.

Selective breeding

For many hundreds of years farmers have used knowledge of the inherited causes of variation to develop particular characteristics in their farm animals and plants. For example, if a farmer wants to improve the quality of the wool produced by his sheep he would choose a ram (male) and ewe (female) that both have the desired quality of wool and breed from them. The offspring that have the best quality wool would then be bred from and so on. So, in each new generation, over many years, this particular characteristic will be bred into the sheep. This is called selective breeding.

The same is true of all farm animals and crops that farmers produce today. Characteristics such as rapid weight gain in pigs and the size and flavour of apples can be bred for in the same way.

! REMEMBER
Selective breeding is when farmers and plant growers decide which characteristics they want a particular animal or plant to have and choose animals or plants with those characteristics to breed from.

Classification of plants and animals

All living things on the Earth can be classified into five kingdoms. These are:

- plants
- animals
- prokaryotes (which include bacteria)
- protista (single-celled animals)
- fungi.

We are most familiar with the first two of these, the plant kingdom and the animal kingdom. The branching diagram below shows how the plant kingdom is divided up. The first two large groups within this kingdom are plants that produce seeds and those that do not produce seeds. The plants that produce seeds belong to one of two groups – either flowering plants or conifers.

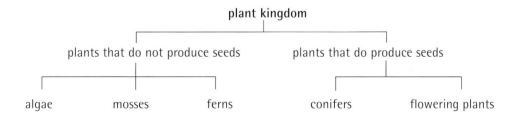

This branching diagram shows the major groups of the animal kingdom. The first feature that divides members of the animal kingdom is whether or not the animal has a backbone. Animals that have a backbone are called vertebrates and animals that do not have a backbone are called invertebrates.

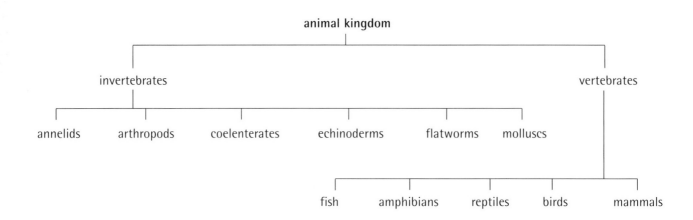

Some words you should know

Species

a group of living things with many similar features, which can successfully interbreed

Classification

the sorting of living things into groups with similar features

Variation

differences between individuals

Inheritance

the passing of genetic information from parent to offspring

The features of vertebrates

Group	Features they have in common
Fish	have fins, gills and scales
Amphibians	live on land and in water; have smooth, damp skin and lay soft eggs in water
Reptiles	have hard dry scales and lay soft-shelled eggs on land
Birds	have feathers and lay hard-shelled eggs on land
Mammals	have hair or fur and feed young on mother's milk

Practice question – Variation and classification

a) The drawings below show a stoat in summer and in winter.

stoat in summer   stoat in winter

In winter the ground is often covered by snow or frost. During this part of the year a stoat's fur is white. Suggest **two** ways its white coat helps a stoat to survive in the winter.

2 marks

b) The diagram shows the family tree for a group of rabbits.

Use words from the list below the diagram to complete the sentences.

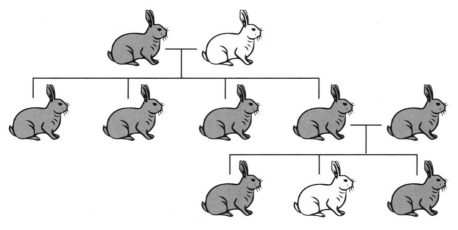

adapt   cytoplasm   genes   grow   inherit
letters   membrane   mutate   nuclei

Rabbits have the same fur all year round.

Young rabbits _____ fur colour from their parents.

Information about fur colour is passed on from one generation to the next in the form of _____ in the

_____ of an egg and sperm.

3 marks

This section is about

- how habitats can support different plants and animals

- how plants and animals survive changes in their habitat

- factors that affect the size of populations within a habitat

- feeding relationships within a particular habitat

- how feeding relationships can be summarised and represented

Habitat and environment

The habitat of a plant or animal is the place where it normally lives. Habitats can be very different. A freshwater pond, a rocky seashore, dense woodland and open moorland are all examples of different habitats. They differ because some are wet, some are light, some are windy and some have other conditions particular to them.

Adapting to change

REMEMBER
In some habitats food may be very scarce during the winter months. Some animals in these habitats hibernate through the winter.

Each different habitat has particular plants and animals living there. This is because each species of plant and animal survives well in the particular conditions or environment of that habitat. These conditions are not always constant. There may be seasonal and even daily changes in these conditions. For example, there could be changes in temperature and in the availability of water. The plants and animals that live in any habitat are adapted to survive these changes.

For instance, some flowering plants growing in woodland areas produce seeds and disperse them before the trees come into leaf. The canopy produced by the leaves reduces the amount of light that reaches the plants on the woodland floor – so without sufficient light they would be unable to produce their seeds.

Competition

All plants need light, water and space to survive. All animals need food, water and space to survive. The members of a species need these same things from their habitat. They have to compete with each other to get enough of them.

This limits the number of each species that can survive in a particular habitat. If the amounts of water, light or food in the habitat change, then the number of a particular species will be affected.

For example:

- if a large shrub dies, the amount of light reaching a smaller flowering plant may increase – it can produce more seeds and these will have more room to germinate and to grow

- if a pond dries up the number of animals in the habitat drops because they go elsewhere to drink or die because of the lack of water.

Living things that compete successfully for resources (light, water, space or food) in the habitat are more likely to reproduce successfully. Their offspring are more likely to survive than the offspring of weaker parents who have not competed well enough to obtain the resources they needed.

☉ Food chains and food webs

The size of the population of a particular species in a habitat will be affected by the number of other species, called predators, that eat it for food. The population of a particular plant will be affected by the number of herbivores and omnivores that feed on it.

The feeding relationships in a habitat can be illustrated by a food web, such as the one below for a seashore. This shows the links between individual food chains in which a producer or consumer may be eaten by more than one other consumer.

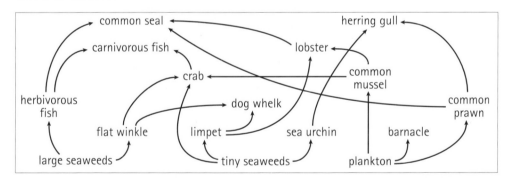

Food chains link together to make a food web

Food webs show which organisms eat others for food. They do not give any information about the numbers of particular plants and animals in any one specific part of the food web or a food chain. The size of the population at each stage in a food chain can be summarised using a pyramid of numbers.

Pyramids of numbers for two food chains

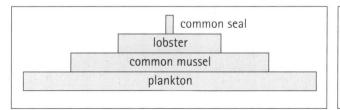

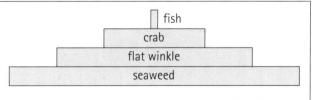

The size of each layer in the pyramid represents the number of each organism at that point in the food chain. In general, the number of organisms decreases towards the top of the pyramid.

Poisons and food chains

Sometimes, toxic (poisonous) substances, such as insecticides, get into a food chain. The plants and animals near the start of a food chain are usually unharmed by the relatively low concentrations of the poison inside them. The poison can become more concentrated in the bodies of animals further up the food chain. Large animals eat many smaller animals, so they take in large quantities of the poison. It may be impossible for the large animals to get rid of the poison, so the amount in their bodies can build up until they die from its effects.

Some words you should know

Word	Meaning
Biomass	cell material made in a green plant by photosynthesis
Carnivore	an animal that only eats other animals
Herbivore	an animal that only eats plants
Omnivore	an animal that eats both plants and animals
Producer	an organism, usually a plant, that makes its own biomass
Consumer	an organism that feeds on a producer or another consumer
Predator	an animal that kills and eats other animals
Prey	an animal that is killed for food by another animal

Key ideas

- Different habitats support different populations of plants and animals.
- Organisms that live in a particular habitat are adapted to survive its daily and seasonal changes.
- Living things in a habitat compete for the resources needed to survive.
- Food chains, food webs and pyramids of numbers can represent the feeding relationships in a habitat.

Practice question – Living things in their environment

In the left-hand column there are descriptions of four food chains (A–D).

In the right-hand column there are four pyramids of numbers (1–4) (not drawn to scale).

Which food chain matches which pyramid of numbers?

4 marks

Description of food chain   **Pyramid of numbers**

A Arthropods feed on tiny algae.

   Sardines feed on tiny arthropods.

   Dolphins feed on sardines.

1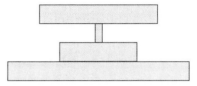

B Antelope feed on grass.

   Lions feed on antelope.

   Fleas live on lions and suck their blood.

2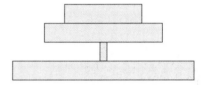

C Greenfly feed on rose bushes.

   Ladybirds feed on greenfly.

   Swallows feed on ladybirds.

3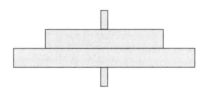

D Zebras feed on long grass.

   Ticks suck the blood of zebras.

   Birds sit on the zebra's backs and eat the ticks.

4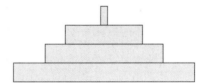

Classifying materials

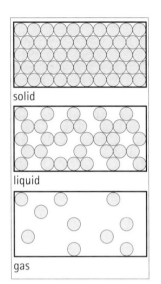

Arrangement of particles in a solid, a liquid and a gas

solid

liquid

gas

This section is about

- the particle model of matter

- how the particle model explains the properties of matter

- how elements are defined, represented and shown in the periodic table

- how compounds are formed, composed and represented

- techniques used to separate mixtures into their constituents

📺 💿 Solid, liquid and gas

All matter can exist in three states: solid, liquid and gas. The arrangement of particles in each of the states of matter is shown in the diagrams on the left and described in the table below.

	Solids	Liquids	Gases
Arrangement of particles	in a fixed regular pattern	irregular	irregular
Forces between particles	strong forces	strong forces	very weak forces
Movement of particles	particles vibrate in a fixed position	move freely but quite slowly	very fast and random
Distance between particles	very close together	close together	far apart

The ideas in the particle model can explain the properties of the three states of matter. For example, solids have a fixed shape, are hard to compress and do not flow. This is because solids are made up of particles that are in a fixed regular pattern, very close together and held together by strong forces. The properties of both liquids and gases can be explained in the same way. Changing the temperature of a substance can cause a change of state.

Summary of changes of state

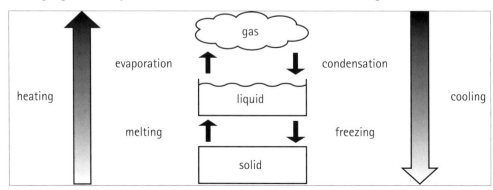

The particle model can be used to explain what happens during each of these changes of state. Melting and evaporation can be used as examples.

Melting

The thermal energy given to the solid makes the particles vibrate faster and more violently until the forces holding the particles together break. The particles can then flow away from the fixed pattern because they have become part of a liquid (see diagram below).

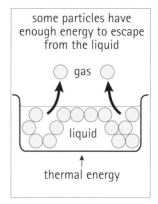

Evaporation

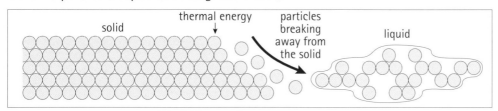

Melting

Evaporation

The thermal energy given to the liquid makes the particles move faster. Some of the particles close to the surface of the water will have enough energy to travel upwards and escape from the surface of the liquid into the air above (see diagram, top right).

Other properties of the states of matter can also be explained by the particle model. The pressure that a gas exerts on the inside of any container it is held in is caused by the collisions between the gas particles and the sides of the container (see diagram on right). The pressure will change if the number of collisions changes or the speed at which the particles are travelling changes.

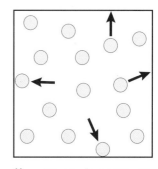

How gas exerts a pressure

The movement of particles to fill all the available space or to move between particles of another substance is called diffusion. For example, the particles of a substance which has a distinct smell move away from the substance, because air particles collide with them and move them about (see below).

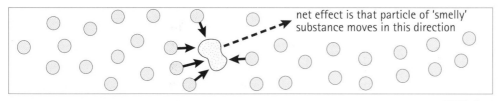

Diffusion

☉ Atoms and molecules

All matter is made up of tiny particles called atoms. Atoms consist of a small, heavy nucleus containing protons and neutrons surrounded by orbiting electrons. Each different atom has a different number of protons.

When two or more atoms are chemically joined together they form a molecule. A molecule can be a combination of the same type of atom. For example, H_2 is a molecule of hydrogen gas, which is two hydrogen atoms joined together (see diagram on right). Molecules can also be a combination

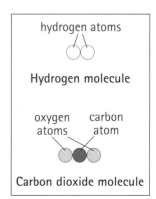

Arrangement of atoms in hydrogen and carbon dioxide

of the atoms of two or more different elements. For example, CO_2 is the molecule of carbon dioxide, which is one atom of carbon joined to two atoms of oxygen (see diagram at bottom of page 33).

☎ ◉ Elements, compounds and mixtures

Elements

Element	Symbol
Iron	Fe
Carbon	C
Magnesium	Mg
Oxygen	O
Calcium	Ca
Hydrogen	H
Copper	Cu
Silicon	Si
Titanium	Ti
Neon	Ne
Tin	Sn
Sulphur	S

Some common elements

A substance made up of just one type of atom is called an element. This means that elements are pure substances that cannot be split up into simpler substances. There are just over 100 different elements that make up all matter. Some common elements are listed in the table on the left.

Elements:

- can be represented by a symbol, for example C for carbon, O for oxygen
- are all shown in the periodic table (see page 36)
- are made up of atoms that all have the same number of protons
- have a number in the periodic table that is the number of protons in their atoms
- can combine together in chemical reactions to form compounds.

Compounds

Most of the substances around you contain more than one element. Compounds are substances made up of the atoms of two or more different elements that have joined together during a chemical reaction.

Compounds:

- have chemical properties that are different to the elements of which they are made
- can be represented by a formula, for example H_2O for water, NaCl for sodium chloride
- are chemical combinations of elements in fixed proportions. The number after the symbol of each element is the number of atoms that combine in that compound. Ethane has the formula C_2H_4 – two atoms of carbon combined with four atoms of hydrogen.

Mixtures

A compound is a chemical combination of different elements. A mixture is a combination of substances that are not chemically combined. This means that the substances in the mixture can be separated. Mixtures can be separated by a range of different methods, shown on page 35.

Filtration

is used to separate insoluble solids from liquids, for example the separation of sand from a sugar solution.

Evaporation

is used to separate soluble solids from their solvent, for example the separation of copper sulphate from water.

Distillation

is used to separate a soluble solid from a liquid or a mixture of liquids, for example the separation of vinegar from water.

Fractional distillation

is used to separate a mixture of liquids that have different boiling points, for example the separation of the hydrocarbons in crude oil.

Chromatography

is used to separate a mixture of different coloured dyes, for example the separation of the different colours in a sample of ink.

Methods of separation

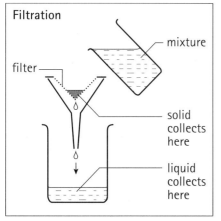

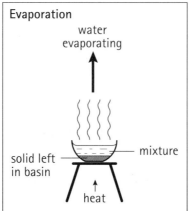

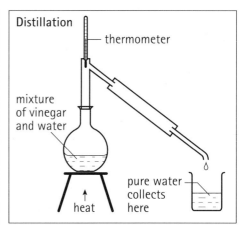

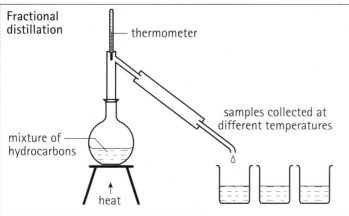

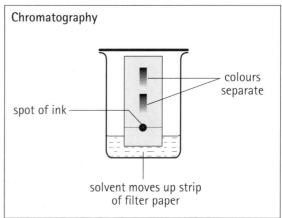

The periodic table of the
elements

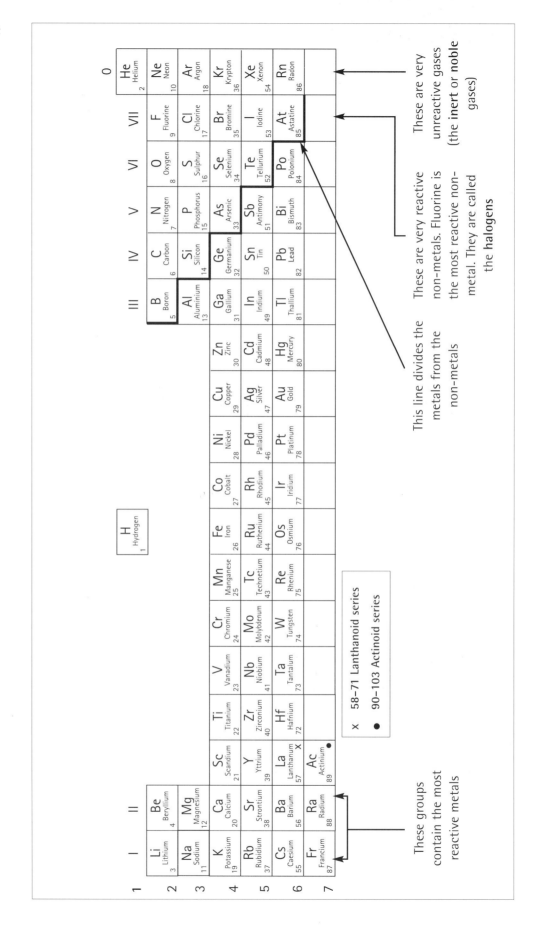

Some words you should know

<u>Model</u>

a set of ideas that help us to understand what happens to things that we cannot observe directly

<u>Pure substance</u>

a substance that is not a mixture. It contains one element or compound only

Practice question – Classifying materials

A section of the periodic table of elements is shown below.

1	I	II			H Hydrogen 1		III	IV	V	VI	VII	He Helium 2
2	Li Lithium 3	Be Beryllium 4					B Boron 5	C Carbon 6	N Nitrogen 7	O Oxygen 8	F Fluorine 9	Ne Neon 10
3	Na Sodium 11	Mg Magnesium 12					Al Aluminium 13	Si Silicon 14	P Phosphorus 15	S Sulphur 16	Cl Chlorine 17	Ar Argon 18

a) Where in this section of the periodic table are the metals found?   *1 mark*

b) Sodium chloride is formed when sodium and chlorine combine together in a chemical reaction.

   Write the symbols for sodium and chlorine.   *2 marks*

c) The formula for a substance is MgS. What is the name of this substance?   *1 mark*

d) Give the name of ONE element in the table that is a gas at room temperature and in which the atoms are joined together in molecules.   *1 mark*

Changing materials

This section is about

- what happens during physical change

- dissolving and solubility

- expansion and contraction

- the weathering of rocks

- the three classes of rock and how each is formed

⊕ ◉ Physical change

REMEMBER Even though a substance might look very different after a physical change its mass is exactly the same as it was before the change.

At room temperature, about 20°C, oxygen is a gas, water is a liquid and aluminium is a solid. This is because all substances change state at different temperatures. The melting and boiling temperatures for these three substances are shown in the table below:

Name	Melting temperature °C	Boiling temperature °C
oxygen	-218	-183
water	0	100
aluminium	660	2467

Melting and boiling are both examples of a change of state. A change of state is one type of physical change. A change of state:

- does not produce a new substance

- requires thermal energy to be taken in or given out

- can be easily reversed.

Other types of physical change also take place when:

- the form of a solid is changed without a change of state, for example when marble rock is crushed to marble chips

- substances expand or contract

- one substance dissolves in another.

ⓉⓋ ◉ Dissolving

When one substance dissolves in another a mixture called a solution is formed. The substance that is dissolved is called the solute and the substance that it dissolves into is called the solvent. Solutes can be solids, liquids and gases but solvents are usually liquids.

Solubility

The solubility of a substance is a measure of how soluble it is in a particular solvent. This can be calculated by finding the maximum mass of the substance that can be dissolved in 100g of water at a particular temperature. When the maximum mass of solute is dissolved in a solvent, no more solute can be dissolved and the solution is called a saturated solution.

The solubility of:

- different solutes at the same temperature is very different
- the same solute is different at different temperatures
- the same solute is different in different solvents.

ⓉⓋ ◉ Expansion and contraction

When most objects are heated they expand (get bigger) and when objects are cooled they contract (get smaller). By supplying thermal energy to the particles of an object they can move further apart (see diagram on right). In liquids and gases the particles can move apart freely, but even in solids the particles are able to vibrate more vigorously and move further apart.

The force exerted by any object as it expands or contracts can be considerable. Lengths of railway track would buckle on hot summer days if there were not gaps between them to allow for expansion. Lengths of overhead telephone cable would break on cold winter days if they were hung without a slight sag to allow for contraction.

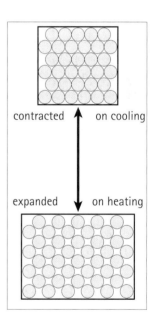

Expansion and contraction of a solid

Weathering of rocks

Water is the only substance that does not contract when it freezes. As it cools from 4°C to 0°C water expands. The forces exerted when water in a crack of a rock freezes can be enough to break large rocks into smaller ones.

When rocks are broken down by the freezing of water, it is called weathering. Once inside the crack, the water will expand as it freezes if the temperature falls to 0°C. As it expands, the water exerts a force on the rock large enough to push it part. If this happens again and again, pieces will break away from the rock (see diagram on page 40).

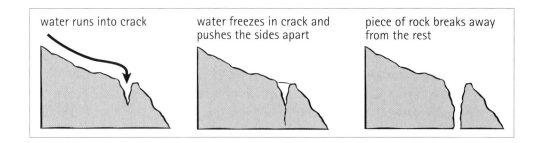

water runs into crack

water freezes in crack and pushes the sides apart

piece of rock breaks away from the rest

Rocks can also be weathered by continual expansion and contraction because of changes in the temperature of their surroundings. Rocks in the desert get very hot during the day and very cold at night. Over long periods the expansion during the day and the contraction during the night create forces within the rocks that cause them to break up.

📺 ⊙ Types of rock

There are three different groups of rocks – sedimentary, metamorphic and igneous. Each type of rock is different because of the way it was formed. The recycling of all existing rocks to form new rocks takes millions of years. The process is summarised in the rock cycle table and diagram below.

Rock type	Formation	Appearance	Examples
Sedimentary	Sediments fall to the bottom of the sea and are compressed together by the weight of the sediments above	Layered and often contain fossils	Limestone, sandstone
Igneous	When molten rock from inside the Earth (magma) cools	Interlocking crystals of different sizes. No layers can be seen	Granite, basalt
Metamorphic	Existing rocks are changed by high temperatures or high pressures	Crystalline with streaks or layers	Marble, slate

The rock cycle

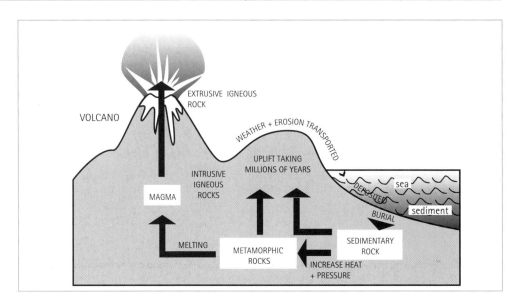

Some words you should know

Weathering

the action of physical or chemical processes that break rocks and minerals into smaller pieces

Key ideas

■ Mass is conserved (stays the same) during a physical change.

■ Solubility is a measure of how soluble a solute is in a particular solvent.

■ The rock cycle explains how existing rocks are recycled to form new rocks.

■ The process of formation for each of the three rock types is different and this accounts for the physical and chemical differences between them.

Practice question – Changing materials

Some crushed ice at -20°C was placed in a beaker. A thermometer was put into the ice and the beaker was warmed for 15 minutes.

The graph shows how the reading on the thermometer changed over the 15 minutes.

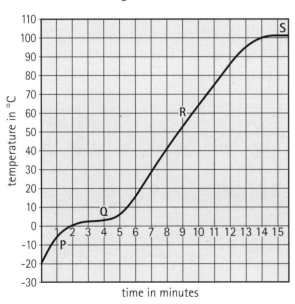

a) By how many degrees Celsius did the temperature in the beaker change during the 15 minutes?

1 mark

b) Which letter on the graph shows:

  i) when the ice is melting?

  ii) when the water is boiling?

2 marks

c) During the experiment, the beaker and its contents were quicky removed from the heat and weighed on a balance at the following times:

at 0 minutes

at 5 minutes

at 10 minutes

at 15 minutes

  i) At which TWO times would you expect the readings on the balance to be the same?

1 mark

  ii) Between which TWO of these times was the mass of the contents of the beaker changing most rapidly?

1 mark

Chemical reactions

This section is about

- how word equations can represent chemical reactions

- different types of chemical reaction

- the production of metals from metal oxides

- some chemical reactions that are not generally useful

- the production of energy from burning fuels and the possible effects on the environment

! REMEMBER During a chemical reaction the total mass of the reactants is always equal to the total mass of the products.

In chemical reactions the substances that react – the reactants – are changed into new substances called products. Most materials that people use are produced by chemical reactions.

Word equations

Each chemical reaction can be represented by a word equation. This uses the names of the chemicals involved and shows which substances react to form which products. The general form of a word equation is this:

reactant + reactant $\longrightarrow$ product + product

An example for the reaction between calcium and water is:

calcium + water $\longrightarrow$ calcium hydroxide + hydrogen

📺 ◉ Types of reaction

There are many different types of chemical reaction.

Oxidation reactions

These are reactions where oxygen is gained by one of the reactants. For example, aluminium reacts with oxygen in the air to form aluminium oxide:

aluminium + oxygen $\longrightarrow$ aluminium oxide

Combustion reactions

These are oxidation reactions that release large quantities of thermal energy. For example, when a fuel burns it produces water and carbon dioxide with the release of energy:

$$\text{fuel} + \text{oxygen} \xrightarrow{\text{energy released}} \text{water} + \text{carbon dioxide}$$

Thermal decomposition reactions

These are reactions where substances decompose when they are heated. For example, calcium carbonate decomposes to calcium oxide and carbon dioxide when it is heated:

calcium carbonate $\longrightarrow$ calcium oxide + carbon dioxide

Displacement reactions

These are reactions where one metal displaces another from a compound. For example, magnesium displaces copper in this reaction:

magnesium + copper sulphate $\longrightarrow$ magnesium sulphate + copper

Neutralisation reactions

These are reactions where an acid reacts with an alkali to produce a metal salt and water. For example, hydrochloric acid and sodium hydroxide neutralise each other to form sodium chloride and water:

hydrochloric acid + sodium hydroxide $\longrightarrow$ sodium chloride + water

Useful reactions

Chemical reactions produce a wide range of useful products. For example, they are used to produce:

- the chemicals used to make plastics
- drugs used as medicines
- cement, used to construct buildings
- cosmetics
- household cleaners.

Making metals

Another very useful group of reactions are those that allow metals to be produced from metal oxides. Metals are materials with a range of uses but they have to be separated from the elements with which they are combined. Iron oxide can be dug from the ground. In a 'blast furnace' the iron oxide will react with carbon monoxide to produce iron and carbon dioxide:

iron oxide + carbon monoxide $\longrightarrow$ iron + carbon dioxide

The iron has lost the oxygen with which it was combined. The iron has been reduced. This sort of reaction, called reduction, is the opposite of oxidation and is used to separate most metals from their oxides.

Unhelpful reactions

Some chemical reactions make products that are not useful. The corrosion of iron and steel is called rusting. Iron reacts with water and oxygen in the air to form iron oxide, which reduces the strength of the iron.

Possible solutions are:

■ to protect the metal by painting

■ to protect the metal by coating with another metal

■ to replace the metal.

Some foods spoil when the chemicals they contain are oxidised by oxygen in the air. Milk turns sour because the fats and oils that it contains are oxidised to compounds that have an unpleasant smell.

Pollution

Combustion reactions produce heat energy. The controlled burning of fossil fuels in power stations is used to drive generators that produce electricity. Electricity is a very convenient and usable energy resource. However, burning fossil fuels can have adverse effects on the environment. Possible effects are:

■ it increases the concentration of carbon dioxide in the atmosphere, which might increase global warming

■ it produces pollutants such as sulphur dioxide, which reacts with water in the atmosphere to fall as 'acid rain'.

FactZONE

Some words you should know

Reactants

the chemicals that react together in a chemical reaction

Products

the chemicals produced during a chemical reaction

Pollutants

chemicals released into the environment that have unpleasant or undesirable effects or are harmful to living things

Key ideas

■ During a chemical reaction mass is conserved.

■ Chemical reactions can be represented and summarised by word equations.

■ There are many types of chemical reaction.

■ Reduction takes place when a reactant in a chemical reaction loses oxygen.

■ Most chemical reactions produce useful substances but some take place that are not useful.

■ The burning of fossil fuels can be controlled to produce electricity but this can have adverse effects on the environment.

Practice question – Chemical reactions

An experiment was set up to investigate rusting. Some clean, shiny iron nails were sealed in a glass bottle containing some tap water. The sealed bottle was then placed on a top-pan balance. The reading on the balance was 549.8g.

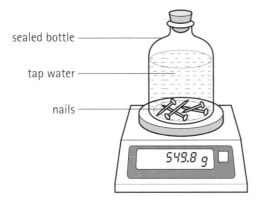

sealed bottle

tap water

nails

549.8 g

The sealed bottle was left for one week. After one week the nails were rusty.

a) i)   What would you expect the reading on the balance to be after one week?

1 mark

ii) Give a reason for your answer.

1 mark

b) i)   Rust is an oxide of iron. Another oxide of iron is iron (III) oxide. Write a word equation for the formation of iron (III) oxide from its elements.

1 mark

ii) Which one of the following words best describes the formation of iron (III) oxide from its elements?

combustion

condensation

decomposition

oxidation

1 mark

Metals and non-metals

This section is about

- the physical properties of non-metallic and metallic elements

- the reactions of metals with oxygen, water and acids

- the reactions between metals and the solutions of salts of other metals

- the reactivity series of metals

Elements can be divided into two groups. The two groups are metals and non-metals. Some examples of each group are shown in the table below.

Metal	Symbol	Non-metal	Symbol
Iron	Fe	Carbon	C
Copper	Cu	Sulphur	S
Magnesium	Mg	Oxygen	O
Aluminium	Al	Chlorine	Cl
Chromium	Cr	Bromine	Br

The physical properties of elements can be used to classify them as either metals or non-metals. The table below summarises the general properties of both groups.

Metals	Non-metals
Usually silvery	Different colours
Good electrical conductors	Poor electrical conductors
Good thermal conductors	Poor thermal conductors
Usually strong	Usually weak
Flexible	Brittle
Shiny	Dull
Usually high melting point	Usually low melting point
Mostly solids at room temperature	Solid, liquid or gas at room temperature
Some are magnetic	None are magnetic

Metals have many properties in common but non-metals are much more varied in their properties. There are some notable exceptions in each group, which have some of the properties of that group but do not have some of the others. For example, mercury is a metal but it is a liquid at room temperature. Carbon is a non-metal but in one form, diamond, it is very strong and in another form, graphite, it is a good conductor of electricity.

📺 💿 Reactions with metals

Metals take part in many important chemical reactions. The reactions between metals and oxygen, water and acids can be summarised by these equations.

Reaction with oxygen

General   metal + oxygen $\longrightarrow$ metal oxide

Example   magnesium + oxygen $\longrightarrow$ magnesium oxide

Symbols $2Mg + O_2 \longrightarrow 2MgO$

Reaction with water

General   metal + water $\longrightarrow$ metal hydroxide + hydrogen

Example   potassium + water $\longrightarrow$ potassium hydroxide + hydrogen

Symbols $2K + 2H_2O \longrightarrow 2KOH + H_2$

Reaction with acid

General   metal + acid $\longrightarrow$ metal salt + hydrogen

Example   zinc + hydrochloric acid $\longrightarrow$ zinc chloride + hydrogen

Symbol $Zn + 2HCl \longrightarrow ZnCl_2 + H_2$

📺 💿 The reactivity series

The speed and violence of each of these reactions is different for different metals. Some metals react very rapidly and others do not react at all. This is because some metals are more reactive than others. The reactivity series of metals lists them according to how well they react in different conditions.

The reactivity series can be worked out from the results of a number of displacement reactions. If a metal, A, is placed into a solution of a salt of metal B, a reaction will take place if A is more reactive than B. A will replace B in the salt. If A is less reactive than B, no reaction will take place. For example, when a piece of iron is placed in a solution of copper sulphate it becomes covered with a thin layer of copper. This can be summarised by a word equation:

$$\text{iron} + \text{copper sulphate} \longrightarrow \text{iron sulphate} + \text{copper}$$

The copper has been replaced by iron in the compound. Iron must be more reactive than copper, so is higher in the reactivity series. The table below shows the reactivity series of common elements.

! **R E M E M B E R**
The non-metals carbon and hydrogen (shown in *italics*) are included in the reactivity series because they both react with some metals but not with others.

Metal	Symbol	
Potassium	K	Most reactive
Sodium	Na	
Calcium	Ca	
Magnesium	Mg	
Aluminium	Al	
Carbon	C	
Zinc	Zn	Increasing reactivity
Iron	Fe	
Tin	Sn	
Lead	Pb	
Hydrogen	H	
Copper	Cu	
Silver	Ag	
Gold	Au	Least reactive

The metals follow the same order of reactivity in all of their reactions. Because of this it's possible to make predictions about the reactions of metals with other substances. By using differences in reactivity you can predict that:

■ zinc will displace lead from lead nitrate

■ calcium will displace magnesium from magnesium sulphate.

FactZONE

Key ideas

■ Metals and non-metals have different physical properties.

■ Different metals react at different rates with oxygen, water and acids.

■ A reaction where one metal replaces a less reactive metal is called a displacement reaction.

■ The reactivity series lists metals in order of their reactivity, the most reactive at the top and the least reactive at the bottom.

Practice question – Metals and non-metals

The table below shows the observations made when four metals are added to cold water and to hydrochloric acid.

Metal	Observations with cold water	Observations with dilute hydrochloric acid
zinc	no reaction	bubbles of gas form and the metal slowly dissolves
platinum	no reaction	no reaction
potassium	the metal floats and then melts, a flame appears and sometimes there is an explosion	(cannot be done safely)
nickel	no reaction	a few bubbles of gas form if the acid is warmed

a) Write the names of these four metals in the order of their reactivity, starting with the most reactive.   *1 mark*

b) i) Give the name of another metal, **not** in the table, that reacts in a similar way to potassium.

   ii) What gas is formed when zinc reacts with dilute hydrochloric acid?

   iii) The experiment with potassium and dilute hydrochloric acid should **not** be done in school laboratories. Suggest why it is dangerous.   *3 marks*

c) A scientist set up two test tubes as shown below.

   In test tube B the zinc strip was slowly covered with a grey deposit. Nothing happened in the other test tube.

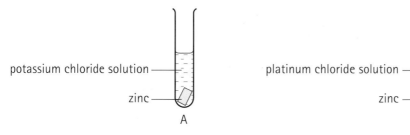

potassium chloride solution ———| |
zinc ———|
A

platinum chloride solution ———| |
zinc ———|
B

   i)   What was the grey deposit in test tube B?

   ii) Why was this grey deposit formed in test tube B?

   iii) Explain why **no** reaction took place in test tube A.   *3 marks*

Acids and alkalis

This section is about

- defining acids and alkalis and identifying examples of each
- how indicators can be used to classify solutions
- the pH scale
- the reactions of acids with metals and with bases
- neutralisation

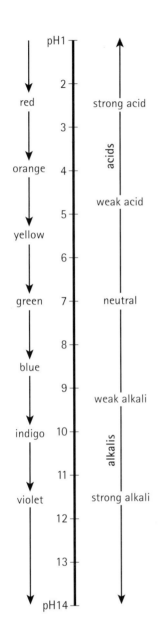

Diagram to show colour changes of Universal Indicator with solutions of different pH

Vinegar, oranges and grapefruit juice all contain acids. You will have heard of hydrochloric acid and sulphuric acid. All acids contain the element hydrogen and react in the same ways with substances such as metals and alkalis. Alkalis are produced when bases (metal oxides) dissolve in water. Many soaps, oven cleaner and washing powder contain alkalis. Solutions of sodium hydroxide and calcium hydroxide are examples of alkalis that you may have come across. Liquids that are neither acidic nor alkaline are neutral. Water is an example of a neutral liquid.

Indicators

Indicators can be used to classify liquids or solutions as acidic, neutral or alkaline. A common indicator is litmus. Litmus remains unchanged in a neutral solution, turns red in an acidic solution and turns blue in an alkaline solution.

An indicator called Universal Indicator can be used to measure the acidity or alkalinity of a solution. Universal Indicator is a mixture of several dyes extracted from plants. The overall colour of the indicator in the solution is compared with the range of colours in the pH scale to give a measure of acidity or alkalinity of the solution (see chart on left).

A neutral solution has a pH of 7. A solution with a pH less than 7 is acidic, with the strongest acids having the lowest pH value. A solution with a pH greater than 7 is alkaline, with the strongest alkalis having the highest pH value.

⊕ ◉ Acids

Acids take part in some important chemical reactions. The reactions between acids and metals are all very similar and can be summarised in this word equation:

metal + acid ⟶ metal salt + hydrogen

For example:

magnesium + sulphuric acid ⟶ magnesium sulphate + hydrogen

The reaction of acids and metal carbonates can be summarised in this word equation:

acid + metal carbonate ⟶ metal salt + carbon dioxide + water

For example:

sulphuric + sodium ⟶ sodium + carbon + water
acid   carbonate   sulphate   dioxide

The reaction of acids with alkalis can be summarised in this word equation:

acid + alkali ⟶ metal salt + water

For example:

sulphuric acid + potassium hydroxide ⟶ potassium sulphate + water

Neutralisation

Reactions between acids and alkalis are called neutralisation reactions. Sulphuric acid and potassium hydroxide neutralise each other. This means that the resulting solution is neutral and has a pH of 7. People put this to use in many ways. Excess stomach acid can cause the pain we call indigestion. Medicines that cure indigestion are called antacids and are weak alkalis. By taking magnesium hydroxide in water the excess stomach acid can be neutralised. Also, farmers add lime (calcium hydroxide) to soil to neutralise excess acidity, which might otherwise prevent their crops from growing.

Harmful reactions

Sulphur dioxide and nitrogen dioxide are gases produced by power stations and some factories. In the air they react with water to form weak solutions of sulphuric acid and nitric acid. This solution might eventually fall as acid rain, which can have the following effects:

- corrosion of metals exposed to the air
- the chemical weathering of rocks
- washing nutrient salts out of top soil
- increasing the acidity of rivers and lakes.

Some words you should know

Base

a substance that reacts with an acid to form a salt and water as the only products

Acid

compound containing the element hydrogen

Alkali

a solution of a base

Salt

a compound in which hydrogen atoms of an acid have been replaced by metal atoms

Neutralisation

the reaction between an acid and an alkali to form a salt and water

Key ideas

- Many common substances contain either acids or alkalis.

- Universal Indicator is used to show the strength of acids and alkalis. A neutral solution has pH7. Acids have pH values less than 7. Alkalis have pH values greater than 7.

- Reactions between acids and alkalis are called neutralisation reactions. These can be summarised by the word equation:

  acid + alkali $\longrightarrow$ salt + water

- Acids can have some useful effects, such as curing indigestion and neutralising alkaline soil. They also produce acid rain, which is harmful to the environment.

Practice question – Acids and alkalis

The table below shows the pH value of five soil samples.

Soil sample	pH of soil
A	6.0
B	7.5
C	7.0
D	4.5
E	8.0

Use letters from the table to answer questions a) and b).

a) Which soil sample is neutral?   *1 mark*

b) i) Most types of heather grow better in acidic soil. In which of the soil samples should heather grow well?   *1 mark*

   ii) Cabbage grows better in alkaline soil. In which of the soil samples should cabbage grow well?   *1 mark*

c) Lime is an alkaline substance that is sometimes put onto acidic soils. What type of reaction takes place between the lime and the acid?   *1 mark*

This section is about

- electrical charge and static electricity

- electrical current in circuits

- the magnetic field around a bar magnet

- electromagnets

Electrical charge

When some materials are rubbed together they become charged. The friction between the two materials causes electrons to be removed from one of them and added to the other. Because electrons carry a negative charge, when a material gains electrons it becomes negatively charged. The material that loses the electrons becomes positively charged. These charges stay where they are produced if the material is an insulator and create 'static electricity'.

Objects with similar charges repel each other. Objects with opposite charges attract each other. This happens because of the forces that charges exert on each other.

If the material on which the charges are produced is a conductor the charges will flow away from the point where they were produced. This is because they can move freely though materials such as metals, which are good conductors. The flow of charged particles through a conductor is called electrical current.

The electrical current that flows around an electric circuit is also a flow of charged particles. These charges transfer energy from a battery or other power supply to the components in the circuit. The current is measured in amps (symbol A), using an ammeter. The current that leaves a component such as a lamp or a motor is the same as the current that enters it.

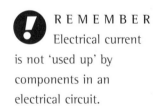

REMEMBER Electrical current is not 'used up' by components in an electrical circuit.

Circuits

There are two different types of electrical circuit: series and parallel.

In a series circuit (see diagram at top of page 54):

- there is only one path that the current can take between the two terminals of the power supply

A series circuit

The switch turns on or off all of the components in the circuit. The current is the same at every point in the circuit.

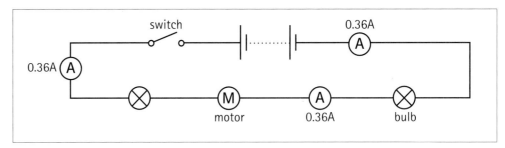

- a switch placed anywhere in the circuit will turn on or off all of the components in the circuit

- the current is the same at all points in the circuit – the reading on an ammeter connected anywhere in the circuit will be the same

- the size of the current that passes through the circuit depends on the number of cells in the battery (or the voltage of the power supply) and the number and type of components in the circuit

- increasing the number of cells in the circuit (or the voltage of the power supply) will increase the current, but adding more components (bulbs, motors or buzzers) will reduce the current because there is more resistance in the circuit.

In a parallel circuit (see diagram on left):

- there is more than one path the current can take between the terminals of the power supply

- a switch in a parallel circuit will only turn on or off those components in the same current path

- the current splits and rejoins at the circuit junctions. At each junction the total current entering it is the same as the total current leaving it

- the current is not the same in all parts of the circuit. The current in each branch of the circuit will depend on the components in that branch. The current in each branch of the circuit can only be measured by connecting an ammeter into that branch

- the total of the currents in the branches of the circuit is the same as the current between the power supply and a junction.

A parallel circuit

The switch turns on or off only the two bulbs in the centre branch of the circuit. The current is different in different parts of the circuit.

⊞ ◉ Magnetism

The most common magnetic materials are iron, steel and nickel. When a piece of one of these materials is magnetised we call it a magnet. Every magnet has a space around it where it exerts a force on other magnets or pieces of magnetic materials. This is called its magnetic field (see diagram on page 55).

All magnets have two poles, a north pole and a south pole. These are the parts of the magnet where the magnetic force is strongest. Magnets exert forces on other magnets. Opposite magnetic poles (one north pole and one south pole) exert a force of attraction on each other. Similar magnetic poles (two north poles or two south poles) exert a force of repulsion on each other. Magnets always attract unmagnetised magnetic materials.

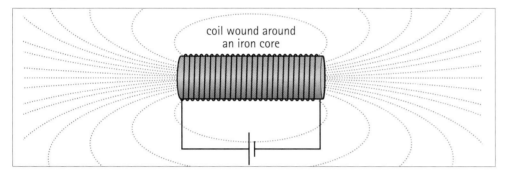

The magnetic field around a bar magnet

Electromagnetism

When an electric current flows through a wire a very weak magnetic field is produced around the wire. If the wire is wound into a coil these magnetic fields add together and look very similar to the field around a bar magnet (see diagram below).

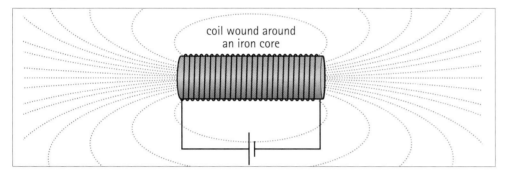

How an electromagnet is formed

If an iron bar is pushed through the middle of the coil, the magnetic field is concentrated into the bar and it behaves like a magnet. The only difference is that when the current is turned off the bar stops being magnetic. This is called an electromagnet. It is a temporary magnet, which means that it is only magnetised while the current is flowing through the coil.

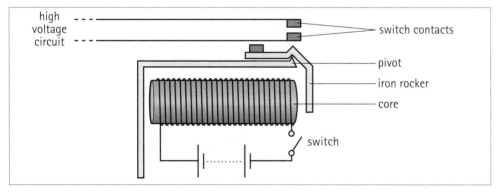

An electromagnetic relay

A relay (see diagram above) is a switch that uses an electromagnet. It is used in circuits where a small current or voltage is used to switch on and off a large current or voltage.

Electromagnets are used in a large number of machines that people use every day. They are used to make loudspeaker cones vibrate, in motors that turn lawn mower blades and for recording onto audiotapes, videotapes and computer disks.

Some words you should know

Conductor

a material that allows either heat or electricity to pass through it easily

Insulator

a material that does not allow either heat or electricity to pass through it easily

Attraction

the force between two objects, pulling them together

Repulsion

the force between two objects, pushing them apart

Friction

is the force that resists the movement of one surface past another

Electrons

the outermost particles within atoms

Charges

particles that are either electrons (negative charges) or particles that have lost electrons (positive charges)

Amp (A)

the unit of electrical current

Key ideas

- Electrons are negatively charged.
- Like charges repel, unlike charges attract.
- The current in a conductor is a flow of electrons.
- The components in an electrical circuit do not 'use up' the current.
- Opposite magnetic poles attract each other, similar magnetic poles repel each other.

Practice question – Electricity and magnetism

The diagram shows a rectangular coil and circuit. It has two iron rods inside it. The rods are parallel and touching. They are free to move.

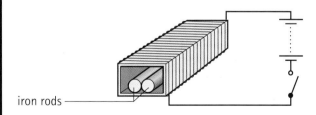

iron rods

a) When the switch is closed, the two rods move apart.

  i) Explain why this happens.   *2 marks*

  ii) The switch is then opened to break the circuit. What, if anything, happens to the two iron rods?   *1 mark*

b) One of the two iron rods is taken out and replaced with a brass rod. The rods are parallel and touching. What, if anything, happens to the rods when the switch is closed? Explain your answer.   *2 marks*

Forces and motion

This section is about

- speed and how to calculate it

- the forces acting on stationary and moving objects

- friction

- forces causing objects to turn about a pivot

- pressure and how to measure it

📺 🔊 Speed

The speed of a moving object is how quickly it moves from one place to another, or the rate at which something is moving. To work out the speed of a moving object you need two measurements: the distance the object travels and the time it takes to move that distance.

You can work out the speed of a moving object by dividing the distance travelled by the time taken. Here is the formula for calculating speed:

$$\text{Speed} = \frac{\text{distance travelled}}{\text{time taken}}$$

The basic unit of speed is the metre per second (m/s).

! REMEMBER
When you work out the speed of a moving object, you measure the distance travelled in metres (m) and the time taken in seconds (s).

Balanced forces

If an object remains stationary or moving in a straight line at a constant speed, as shown in the examples below, the forces acting on it are said to be balanced. If the forces are balanced, then each force acting on the object is cancelled out by another force of equal size acting in the opposite direction.

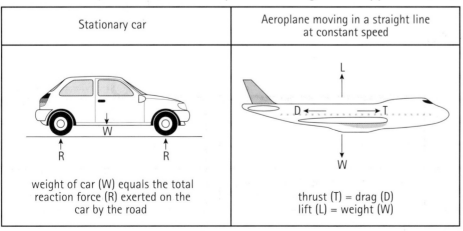

Stationary car	Aeroplane moving in a straight line at constant speed
weight of car (W) equals the total reaction force (R) exerted on the car by the road	thrust (T) = drag (D) lift (L) = weight (W)

Unbalanced forces

If the forces acting on an object are unbalanced, then the speed of the object or the direction in which it is travelling will change. This means that when an object either begins to move or increases its speed, the force in the direction of motion must be greater than the force in the opposite direction. When an object slows down or is brought to a stop, the forces are also unbalanced, but in this case the force opposing the motion is greater than the force in the direction of the motion. This is shown in the diagram below.

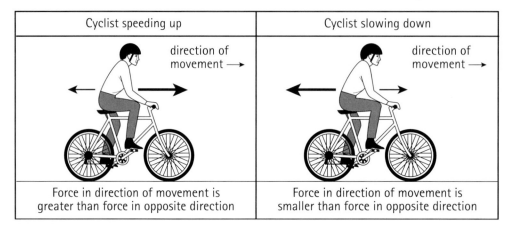

Cyclist speeding up	Cyclist slowing down
Force in direction of movement is greater than force in opposite direction	Force in direction of movement is smaller than force in opposite direction

Friction

REMEMBER The faster an object moves, the greater the air resistance acting on it.

Friction is the force produced when two substances that are touching move past each other. In many cases this is a useful force. Friction is the force that stops your shoes from slipping when you are walking and provides the grip between car tyres and the ground. Friction is also the force that resists the motion of objects when they travel through air, water or over rough surfaces (see diagrams below). When an object moves through the air, it meets air resistance. This is the frictional force that opposes movement through the air.

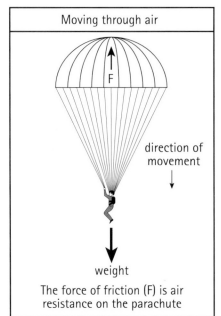

Moving through air

The force of friction (F) is air resistance on the parachute

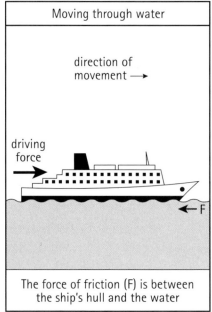

Moving through water

The force of friction (F) is between the ship's hull and the water

Moving over a rough surface

The force of friction (F) is between the rough surface and the car

Turning forces

The point around which an object turns is called the pivot. The object turns because a force is applied to it. The measure of how effective the force is at making an object turn is called the turning effect, or moment, of the force. You can calculate the moment of a force by multiplying the size of the force in newtons (N) by the distance between the force and the pivot in metres (m). Here is the formula for finding a moment:

moment = force x distance from the pivot

The unit used to measure a moment is the newton metre (Nm).

The moment of a force can be increased by:

■ increasing the size of the force, or

■ moving the point of application of the force further from the pivot.

When an object resting on a pivot is not moving it is described as balanced. The moments of the forces on either side of the pivot are equal even though the forces themselves may not be equal.

In the diagram below, the moment on the left is called the anticlockwise moment because it is caused by a force that would turn the plank in that direction. The moment on the right is called the clockwise moment because it is caused by a force that would turn the plank in a clockwise direction.

If there is more than one object exerting a force on either side of the pivot, you work out the moment for each and add them together to find the sum of the moments on that side.

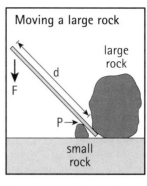

Moving a large rock

The moment of the force (F) around the pivot (P) equals F x d. To increase the moment of the force, either increase the force (F) or use a longer pole to increase d.

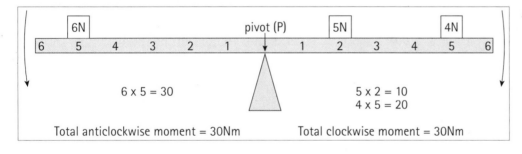

A balanced beam

Pressure

The overall effect of a force on a surface is called pressure. The pressure caused by a force depends on the size of the force and the area over which the force is exerted. You can calculate the pressure on a surface by dividing the force, measured in newtons (N), by the area, measured in square metres (m²). This is the formula to find pressure:

$$\text{Pressure} = \frac{\text{force}}{\text{area}}$$

The unit of pressure is the newton per square metre (N/m²).

To walk on soft surfaces such as snow, your weight needs to be more spread out than when you use ordinary shoes or even boots. Snow shoes reduce the pressure you apply to the snow by providing a large area over which your weight (the force) can be spread.

Low pressure

High pressure

Cutting an apple with a sharp knife is easy because the force you exert is concentrated on a very small area, which means that the pressure you can apply is very high.

FactZONE

Some words you should know

Speed

the rate at which something moves

Force

the push or pull exerted on an object in a particular direction

Friction

the force between two objects or materials as they move past each other

Moment

the effectiveness of a force causing an object to turn about a pivot

Pressure

the effect of a force on an area

Some formulae to know

$$\text{Speed (m/s)} = \frac{\text{distance travelled (m)}}{\text{time taken (s)}}$$

If speed, distance and time are represented by s, d and t, an easy way to remember their relationship is to use this triangle. Cover the one you want to find with your finger and the triangle will show you how to calculate it.

Moment (Nm) = force (N) x distance from the pivot (m)

$$\text{Pressure (N/m}^2) = \frac{\text{force (N)}}{\text{area (m}^2)}$$

If pressure, force and area are represented by P, F and a, an easy way to remember their relationship is to use this triangle:

Key ideas

- When the forces acting on an object are balanced it will stay in its present state of motion, either stationary or moving at constant speed in a straight line.

- When the forces acting on an object are unbalanced they will cause the object to either change shape, change its speed or change its direction, if it is moving.

- The principle of moments states that: when an object resting on a pivot is balanced, the sum of the clockwise moments is equal to the sum of the anticlockwise moments.

- Exerting a force on a small area will produce a high pressure. Spreading the force over a larger area will reduce the pressure.

Practice question – Forces and motion

When a car is being driven along, two horizontal forces affect its motion. One is air resistance and the other is the forward force.

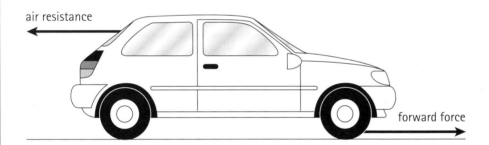

air resistance

forward force

a) i)   Explain how molecules in the air cause air resistance. *1 mark*

   ii) Explain why air resistance is greater when the car is travelling faster. *1 mark*

b) i)   Compare the sizes of the forward force and the air resistance when the car is speeding up. Start your answer with 'The forward force is'. *1 mark*

   ii) Compare the sizes of the two forces while the car is moving at 30 miles per hour. Start your answer with 'The forward force is'. *1 mark*

c) The forward force has to be larger when the car is travelling at a steady 60 mph than when it is travelling at a steady 30 mph. Why is this? *1 mark*

d) The forward force is the result of the tyres NOT being able to spin on the road surface. What is the name of the force that stops the tyres spinning? *1 mark*

Light and sound

This section is about

- comparing light to sound

- the formation of shadows

- reflection and refraction

- dispersion of white light and the colour of objects

- the characteristics of waves

📺 ◉ Light

❗ REMEMBER
Sound waves cannot travel through space because there are no particles to carry the vibrations.

Light travels much faster than sound. In air, sound travels at about 330 metres per second (m/s). Light travels at 300 000 000 m/s, about one million times faster than sound! This is why you can see things before you hear them. Another difference between light and sound is that, because it is a form of radiation, light can travel through space (a vacuum), whereas sound travels as vibrations of the particles of the medium – the solid, liquid or gas – through which it is passing.

Light travels in straight lines and this is the reason why shadows are formed. If light could travel in curved lines or around corners then it would get behind opaque objects and shadows would not be formed.

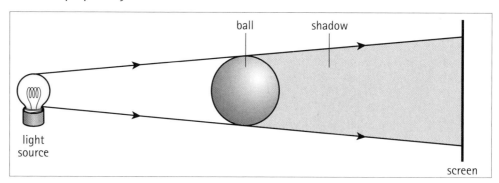

How a shadow is formed

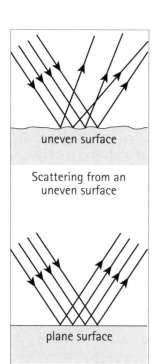

Scattering from an uneven surface

Direct reflection from a plane surface

You can see luminous objects because they produce their own light. Other objects are non-luminous. They reflect some of the light that falls on them, often scattering light in all directions (see diagram on left). You can see these objects because some of the scattered light enters your eyes. Mirrors, however, reflect light in a regular way because of their surface and shape.

Mirrors and reflection

A plane mirror reflects light from its surface at the same angle as the light strikes the surface (see diagram below). This can be summarised by:

the angle of incidence (i) = the angle of reflection (r)

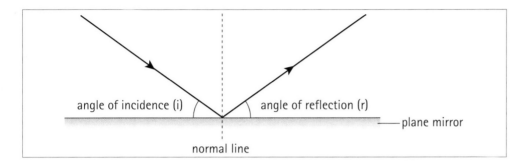

The ray of light striking the mirror is called the incident ray and the ray leaving the mirror is called the reflected ray. The dashed line is called the normal. This is a line at right angles to the point on the mirror where the light strikes it.

Refraction

As light passes from one transparent material to another its speed changes slightly. Light slows down as it passes from air into glass, water or perspex. Light speeds up as it passes out of those materials into the air. If the light passes into and out of one of these materials at right angles to the surface then the light ray passes through with no change of direction (see diagram on right).

If the light passes into or out of a material at an angle then it will change direction as it goes from one material to the other. When the light slows down its direction changes towards the normal line. When the light speeds up, its direction moves away from the normal (see diagram below).

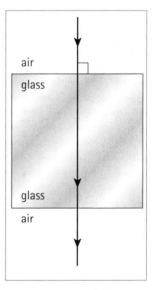

A ray of light striking a glass block at right angles passes through without changing direction

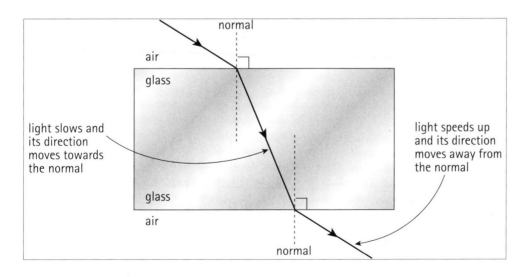

Refraction of white light
through a prism

The process that causes light to change direction when it passes from one
transparent material to another is called refraction. Refraction is often
responsible for distorting what you see. Light is refracted by different
amounts as it passes through frosted glass, for example, so what you see is
quite different to what is actually behind the glass.

Dispersion

White light is a mixture of colours. It contains the colours of the spectrum
(see list on left). When white light passes from air into a block of another
transparent material like glass or perspex the different colours of light are
refracted by different amounts. This makes the white light split up into the
colours of the spectrum. This process is called dispersion.

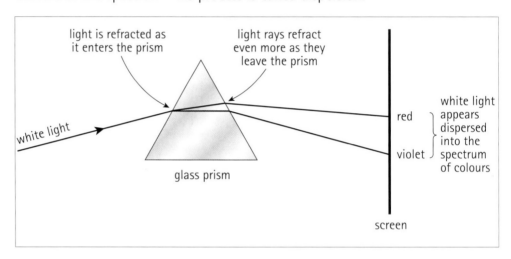

Seeing colours

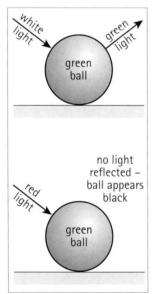

The appearance of a
green ball in white and
red light

Coloured filters are translucent, which means they only allow a specific
colour of light to pass through them. In that way they remove colours from
white light. A red filter will allow red light to pass through but it will absorb
all of the other colours of the spectrum. The only colour of light that you can
see leaving a red filter is red.

When you shine white light onto a green ball, it reflects the green light and
absorbs all of the other colours (see diagram on left). If you shine different
colours of light onto objects they may appear to be different colours. If the
green ball is illuminated by red light there is no green light for it to reflect.
The green ball will appear black because it is absorbing the red light and not
reflecting any light back to your eyes.

📺 Waves

Light and sound both travel from place to place as waves. All waves have
similar features. These features are defined in the table on page 65.

Wave feature	Definition (see diagrams below)
Amplitude	The distance from the central position to the top or bottom of the wave
Frequency	The number of vibrations each second
Wavelength	The length of each complete wave

Frequency is measured in Hertz (Hz) and wavelength is measured in metres (m).

The amplitude of a vibration affects the loudness of the sound that it produces. The larger the amplitude of the vibration the louder is the sound produced. The frequency of a vibration affects the pitch of the sound that it produces. The greater the frequency of a vibration the higher is the pitch of the sound produced.

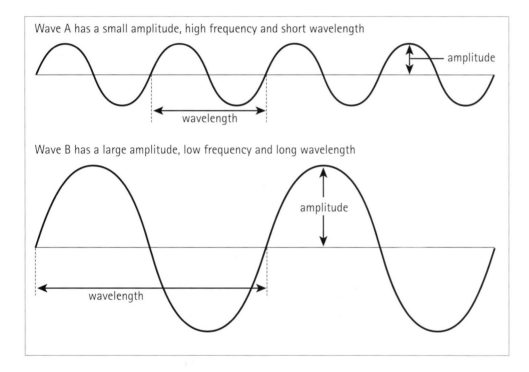

Amplitude, frequency and wavelength

Hearing sounds

You can hear sounds when vibrations in the air make your eardrum vibrate. These vibrations are passed to the inner ear along three small bones called the ossicles. Humans can hear sounds that have frequencies from about 20 Hz to about 20 000 Hz but not everybody can hear across the entire range. Older people may not be able to hear the higher frequencies that younger people can hear.

Very loud sounds can cause damage to the eardrum. It can be stretched by the large amplitude of the vibration causing the sound, which can cause temporary pain and possibly long-term damage.

REMEMBER
Exposure to loud sounds for long periods can result in deafness.

Some words you should know

Vacuum

a space in which there is no matter

Opaque

will not let any light pass through

Luminous

gives out light

Scattering

the reflection of light in every direction

Non-luminous

does not give out light

Spectrum

the range of colours contained within white light

Ossicles

the three small bones of the middle ear

Translucent

will allow some light to pass through

Key ideas

- Light travels in straight lines at a speed much greater than sound.

- The angle of incidence (i) = the angle of reflection (r).

- Refraction occurs when light crosses the boundary between one transparent material and another.

- The spectrum of white light contains seven colours: red, orange, yellow, green, blue, indigo and violet.

- Light and sound are both waves and they have a number of similar features.

Practice question – Light and sound

a) The diagram below shows a ray of red light entering a glass block.

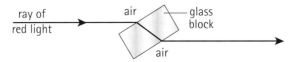

i)   Most of the light goes into the glass block but some does not. What happens to the light that does NOT go into the glass block?   *1 mark*

ii) As the light goes into the glass block it changes direction. What is the name of this effect?   *1 mark*

b) The diagram below shows white light passing through a prism and forming a spectrum of colours on a white screen.

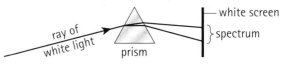

Red is at one end of the spectrum. Write red, blue, green and violet in the order of the spectrum.   *1 mark*

c) A pupil puts a green filter in the ray of white light. What happens to the spectrum on the screen?   *1 mark*

The Earth and beyond

This section is about

- the apparent movement of the Sun in the sky

- the planets in our Solar System

- how we see different objects in the night sky

- the uses of artificial satellites

The Sun is the star at the centre of our Solar System. A star is a massive luminous body that may have planets orbiting around it. The Earth is one of nine planets that orbit the Sun. Gravitational attraction between the planets and the Sun keeps them in orbit. Planets are sometimes visible at night because light from the Sun is reflected from their surface towards the Earth.

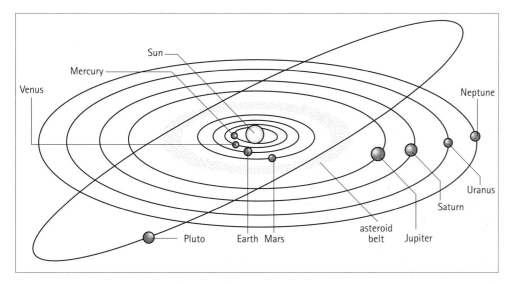

The Solar System

📺 💿 Orbits and cycles

As the Earth orbits the Sun, it rotates on its axis. Because the Earth rotates, it seems to people on Earth that the Sun moves across the sky. It appears to rise in the east and move in an arc across the sky before setting – going below the horizon – in the west. Once the Sun sets you experience night-time.

The Earth makes one complete rotation on its axis each day. This rotation is also the reason why the stars in the night sky seem to rotate daily around the pole star. The stars also seem to change position during the year because the Earth orbits the Sun.

The seasons

The apparent movement of the Sun across the sky varies during the year (see diagram below). The Sun rises higher in the sky in summer than it does in winter. This is because the Earth's axis is tilted.

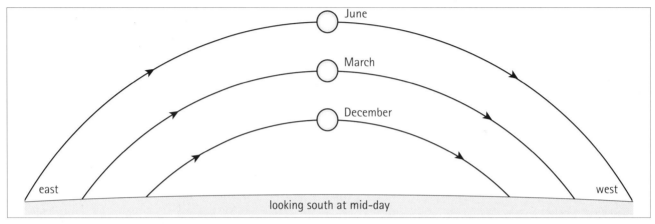

looking south at mid-day

The apparent movement of the Sun across the sky each day at different times of the year

These annual changes are responsible for the different seasons. During summer in the northern hemisphere the Earth is tilted towards the Sun and the days have more hours of daylight than hours of night-time. During the winter in the northern hemisphere the Earth is tilted away from the Sun, and so the days have more hours of night-time than hours of daylight.

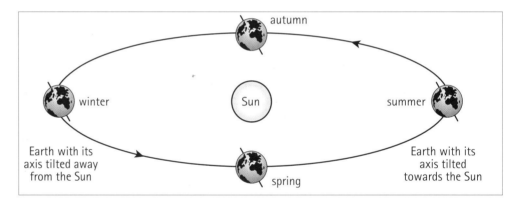

The seasons of the northern hemisphere as the Earth orbits the Sun

📺 Satellites

REMEMBER Just like all other objects in the night sky, the Moon and artificial satellites are visible because they reflect sunlight.

A satellite is a body that orbits a planet. Some of the planets in the Solar System have natural satellites, called moons. The Earth has one natural satellite called the Moon. The Earth also has many artificial satellites. These are machines launched into space and they have many uses:

- collecting information about the weather. These satellites orbit close to the Earth so that they can make several orbits in a day

- communications (telephone, radio and television). Some of these are geostationary. This means that they orbit at the same speed as the Earth turns, so that they remain directly above a particular point on the Earth

- for navigation and for collecting a wide range of information from the Earth's surface.

FactZONE

Some words you should know

Luminous

gives out light

Non-luminous

does not give out light. Reflects light from a luminous source

Year

the time it takes for the Earth to make one complete orbit of the Sun

Northern hemisphere

the half of the Earth north of the equator

Key ideas

- The Sun is the star at the centre of our Solar System. It is luminous and other bodies in the Solar System are visible because they reflect light that comes from the Sun.

- The Earth orbits the Sun once each year. This motion is due to the gravitational attraction between the Earth and the Sun.

- The Earth rotates on its axis once each day. At any time, half of the Earth is in daylight and the other half is in darkness.

- Satellites are bodies that orbit planets. Some planets have natural satellites called moons. As well as our Moon, many artificial satellites orbit the Earth.

Practice question – The Earth and beyond

Mars is the fourth planet from the Sun.

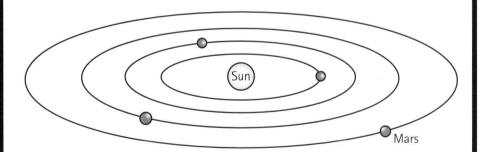

a) Name ONE planet that is closer than Mars to the Sun.   *1 mark*

b) A day and night on Mars lasts nearly 25 Earth hours. Explain why there is daytime and night-time on Mars.   *1 mark*

c) Like Earth, Mars has summers and winters. Suggest why there are seasons on Mars.   *1 mark*

Energy resources and transfer

This section is about

- energy resources and how they were formed

- renewable and non-renewable energy resources

- how electricity is generated

- the different forms of energy

- the transfer and storage of energy

Non-renewable
Coal
Oil
Natural gas
Nuclear

Renewable
Biomass
Wind
Waves
Hydroelectric
Solar
Tidal
Geothermal

Energy resources

Everything that you do requires energy. People use vast quantities of energy to run homes, industries and for transport. Much of the energy used for these purposes is produced by burning fuels such as coal, oil or natural gas. These are called fossil fuels because they were formed from dead plants and animals millions of years ago.

There are many other sources of energy. Some of these are non-renewable – these are energy resources that will eventually be used up because they were formed many millions of years ago and no more are being produced. The others are renewable. These energy resources are always being replaced.

📺 Energy from the Sun

With the exception of tidal, geothermal and nuclear all of the energy resources listed on the left have obtained their energy from the Sun or are constantly available because of energy from the Sun.

- Tidal energy is created by the pull of the Moon on the seas as it moves around the Earth.

- Geothermal energy comes from hot rocks deep inside the Earth's crust.

- Nuclear energy is produced from radioactive materials that are extracted from the Earth's crust.

Biomass is any plant or animal material that is used as a fuel or that is used to produce a fuel. Wood can be burned as a fuel and alcohol, produced from sugar, can be used as a fuel for cars.

📺 Making electricity

All of the energy resources in the list can be used to generate electricity. Most of the electricity, however, is generated by burning fossil fuels.

Electricity has to be produced when it is needed because it cannot be stored in that form. So that its energy can be stored, electricity is used to produce a different energy resource. This can be done in two ways:

■ electricity can be stored as chemical energy in batteries and transferred back into electricity when it is needed

■ electricity can be used to pump large quantities of water from a low reservoir up to a high reservoir behind a dam. The water is a store of potential energy. When the water is allowed to fall down the connecting pipe, its energy of movement – kinetic energy – can be used to drive generators and be transferred back into electricity.

Transducers

Any machine that transfers energy from one form to another is called a transducer. Here are some transducers found in most homes:

Transducer	Transfers energy from	Transfers energy to
television	electrical	light, sound and thermal
microphone	sound	electrical
torch	chemical	light
motor car	chemical	kinetic, thermal and sound
bicycle	chemical (food)	kinetic

In all energy transfers:

■ the total amount of energy before and after the transfer is the same

■ the total amount of usable energy available in the new form will always be less than in the original form

■ some of the energy will be 'lost', or dissipated, when the transfer takes place. This energy will be 'lost' as thermal energy to the surroundings or be used to overcome friction in the workings of the transducer

■ if the amount of dissipated energy can be reduced to a minimum then more of the original energy is available as a resource.

Thermal energy and temperature

The temperature of an object is not a measure of the total amount of energy contained in it. Its temperature is a measure of how hot the object is. A large, cool object, such as a bath of water at 35°C stores much more thermal energy than a small, very hot object like a spark from a sparkler at 2000°C. Although the spark is much hotter than the water in the bath, the amount of energy needed to get it to that temperature is much less.

Some words you should know

<u>Dissipated energy</u>

the unintentional loss of energy during an energy transfer

Key ideas

- Most of the Earth's energy resources originally received their energy from the Sun.

- Non-renewable energy resources will eventually run out.

- Renewable energy resources are always being replaced.

- Everything that happens involves a transfer of energy. The total amount of energy involved remains the same but some of it is wasted because it is 'lost' to the environment.

- The unit of energy is the Joule (J).

Practice question – Energy resources and transfer

Fossil fuels are used to generate electricity but over half of the world's population uses biomass as fuel.

a) What is 'biomass' when it is used as a fuel? *1 mark*

b) Biomass and fossil fuels are both energy resources. What is the original source of this energy? *1 mark*

c) Give the names of THREE fossil fuels that are often burned to generate electricity. *1 mark*

d) Fossil fuels are often described as non-renewable energy resources. Explain why they are often called 'non-renewable'. *1 mark*

e) There are advantages and disdvantages of burning different fuels.

 i) Give ONE advantage of using biomass rather than fossil fuel as an energy resource.

 1 mark

 ii) Give ONE advantage of using fossil fuel rather than biomass as an energy resource.

 1 mark

 iii) Give ONE disadvantage of using both fossil fuel and biomass.

 1 mark

Answers to practice questions

Life processes and cell activities

Page 10

a) Part A is the membrane, part B is the nucleus and part C is the cytoplasm.

b) Plant cells have these parts but animal cells do not: a cell wall, chloroplasts and a large vacuole. Any two from these three will get the marks. You will also get the marks if you give chlorophyll instead of chloroplasts, vacuole instead of large vacuole, or starch grain.

Humans as organisms 1

Page 15

a)

Name of organ system	Letter of the drawing of the organ system
circulatory system	C
digestive system	D
reproductive system	B
respiratory system	A
skeleton	E

b) The reproductive system is the organ system that is completely different in a man and a woman. You will also get the mark if you write B, as this is the letter of the reproductive system in the table.

Humans as organisms 2

Page 19

a) Menstruation is part of a monthly cycle.
The cycle begins when the lining of the uterus breaks away.
An ovum (egg) is released from an ovary at about the middle of each cycle.

b) You will get the marks for describing any two of the following changes to boys' bodies, which occur during adolescence:
- voice becomes deeper or voice breaks or voice changes
- increase in facial hair or grows a beard
- increase in body hair including growth of pubic hair or hairy chest or hair in armpits
- growth of penis or testes or testicles
- start to produce sperm
- growth spurt or rapid growth
- development of a more adult body shape, including wide shoulders
- sweats more.

Green plants as organisms

Page 23

a) i) The ovule becomes the seed.
ii) The ovary becomes the fruit.
iii) The function of the anther is to make or release or store pollen.

b) Goosegrass: the hooks attach it to animals or clothes or fur.
Goat's beard: the hairs or 'parachute' carry it in the wind.
You will only get the marks if you refer to the hooks on the goosegrass fruit and the hairs on the goat's beard fruit.

c) It is an advantage to plants that their seeds are scattered far apart:
- so that they are not crowded
- so that they all get enough nutrients or minerals
- so that they can all get enough water
- so that seedlings are not shaded by the plant or they get enough light
- so that they can grow in new areas
- to reduce the risk of disease spreading.
Any of these will get the mark.

Variation and classification

Page 27

a) The two answers may be in either order.
    Two ways in which its white coat helps a stoat to survive in the winter:
    ■ it helps it to hide from its prey/the animals it eats/rabbits
    ■ it helps it to hide from predators/animals that eat or hunt it
    ■ it is an insulator or it keeps it warm.
    If you write 'to camouflage it', you will only get one mark.

b) Young rabbits inherit fur colour from their parents.
    Information about fur colour is passed on from one generation to the next in the form of genes in the nuclei (or nucleus) of an egg and sperm.

Living things in their environment

Page 31

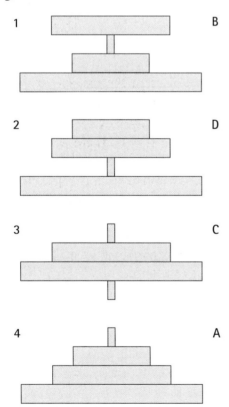

Classifying materials

Page 37

a) In this section of the periodic table the metals are found in columns I, II and III.

b) The symbol for sodium is Na.
    The symbol for chlorine is Cl.

c) Magnesium sulphide is the name of the substance with the formula MgS.

d) All of these elements are gases at room temperature and have atoms that are joined together in molecules: hydrogen, nitrogen, oxygen, fluorine, chlorine.

Changing materials

Page 41

a) The temperature in the beaker rose from -20°C to 101°C. The temperature change during the 15 minutes was 121°C.

b) i) Ice is melting during Q.
    ii) Water is boiling during S.

c) i) The times at which you would expect the two readings on the balance to be the same are 0 minutes and 5 minutes.
    ii) The times between which the mass of the contents of the beaker is changing most rapidly are 10 minutes and 15 minutes.

Chemical reactions

Page 45

a) i) You would expect the reading on the balance after one week to be 549.8g.
    ii) The nails were rusty, a reaction had taken place, but overall mass does not change in a reaction.

b) i) The word equation for this reaction is:
    iron + oxygen $\longrightarrow$ iron (III) oxide
    ii) The formation of iron (III) oxide from its elements is an oxidation reaction.

Metals and non-metals

Page 49

a) Potassium is the only metal that reacts with cold water. It must be more reactive than the other three metals. Platinum does not react with either cold water or dilute hydrochloric acid. It is the least reactive metal. Nickel reacts slowly only if the dilute hydrochloric acid is warmed. Nickel must be less reactive than zinc but more reactive than platinum.

most reactive	potassium
	zinc
	nickel
least reactive	platinum

b) i) Another metal that reacts in a similar way to potassium is sodium or caesium.

ii) The gas hydrogen is formed when zinc reacts with dilute hydrochloric acid.

iii) It is dangerous for this experiment to be done in school laboratories because:
■ the reaction is too violent or it explodes or acid goes everywhere
■ potassium is too reactive.
Either of the above answers will get the mark.

c) i) The grey deposit in test tube B is platinum.

ii) Any one of these answers will get the mark:
■ zinc is more reactive than platinum
■ zinc displaces platinum from the solution
■ platinum is less reactive than zinc.

iii) Either of these answers will get the mark:
■ zinc is less reactive than potassium
■ potassium is more reactive than zinc.

Acids and alkalis

Page 52

a) Soil sample C is neutral.

b) i) Heather should grow well in either of soils A or D.

ii) Cabbage should grow well in either of soils B or E.

c) A neutralisation reaction takes place between lime and the acid.

Electricity and magnetism

Page 56

a) i) The two rods move apart because:
■ the current produces a magnetic field or the coil becomes an electromagnet
■ the rods are magnetised in the same direction
■ the rods repel each other.
You only need give two of these for the two marks.

ii) When the switch is opened, the circuit is broken and the two rods stay apart. If you write that the rods have become demagnetised you will also get the mark.

b) When this experiment is repeated using one brass rod and one iron rod nothing happens. This is because the brass rod does not become magnetised.

Forces and motion

Page 61

a) i) The molecules cause air resistance because they hit the front of the car.

ii) Air resistance is greater when the car is travelling faster because:
■ molecules/particles hit the car faster/harder
■ more molecules/particles hit the car.
Either of the above answers will get the mark.

b) i) The forward force is larger than the air resistance when the car is speeding up .

ii) The forward force is the same as the air resistance when the car is moving at a steady 30 miles per hour.

c) The forward force has to be larger because at 60mph the air resistance is larger or it has to balance the air resistance.

d) The name of the force that stops the tyres spinning is friction.

Light and sound

Page 66

a) i) The light that does not go into the glass block is reflected/bounces off or is scattered or absorbed by the glass.

ii) The name of this effect is refraction.

b) The order of the colours in the spectrum is red, orange, yellow, green, blue, indigo and violet. The order of colours in this list is red, green, blue, violet.

c) The green part of the spectrum stays the same, but the other colours disappear.

The Earth and beyond

Page 69

a) The three planets that are closer than Mars to the Sun are Mercury, Venus and Earth.

b) There is daytime and night-time on Mars because it rotates on its axis.

c) There are seasons on Mars because its axis is tilted.

Energy resources and transfer

Page 72

a) Biomass used as a fuel is material from living things or plant matter.

b) The original source of this energy is the Sun.

c) Three fossil fuels that are often burned to generate electricity are coal, oil and natural gas/methane. Peat will also get the mark.

d) Fossil fuels are called 'non-renewable' because they cannot be replaced or no more can be produced.

e) i) One advantage of using biomass rather than fossil fuel as an energy resource is that it is renewable or it is widely available.

ii) The advantages of using fossil fuel rather than biomass as an energy resource are:

■ it takes up less space or it is more concentrated

■ it is more suitable for use in vehicles or it can be transported more easily

■ it contains more energy per unit mass.

iii) The disadvantages of using both fossil fuel and biomass are:

■ they cause pollution or produce a specific pollutant/carbon dioxide

■ they release greenhouse gases.

Index

acid 50–52

acid rain 51

adapted 8

adolescence 16, 19

air 44

  resistance 58

alcohol 18

alkali 50, 52

alveoli (air sacs) 13

ammeter 53

amp (A) 53, 56

amplitude 65

angle of incidence 63

angle of reflection 63

animal 7, 8, 26

animal kingdom 26

anther 21

antibody 18

artery 18

atom 33

attraction 53, 55, 56

bacteria 18

base 52

battery 53

biomass 70

blood 12, 16

boiling 38

boiling temperature 38

bone 12

breathing 13

bronchi 13

bronchiole 13

capillary 16

carbohydrate 11

carbon dioxide 13, 14, 20

carnivore 30

carpel 21

catalyst 12

cell 8, 9

  animal 8

  electrical 54

  plant 8

  root hair 8, 20

  sap 8

  specialised 8

  sperm 16, 17

cell membrane 8, 9

cell wall 8

characteristics 24

charge 53, 56

chemical reactions 42

chlorophyll 8, 20

chloroplasts 8, 20

chromatography 35

chromosome 24

circuit 53

  parallel 54

  series 53

circuit symbols 54

circulatory system 15

classification 24–26

colour 64

combustion 42, 44

competition 28

compound 34

condensation 32

conductor 53, 56

consumer 29, 30

contraction 39

corrosion 44

cytoplasm 8, 9

daylight 68

decomposition 43

diaphragm 13

diet 11

  balanced 11

diffusion 33

digestion 12

digestive system 15

disease 18

dispersion 64

dissolving 39

distance 57

distillation 35

  fractional 35

drug 18

earth 67, 68, 69

egestion 12, 14

electric charge 53

  circuit 53, 54

  current 53

electricity 53, 70

  static 53

electromagnet 55

electromagnetism 55

electron 33, 53, 56

elements 34, 36

embryo 17

energy 11, 14, 70
   dissipated 71, 72
   kinetic 71
   potential 71
   transfer 71

energy resource 70
   non-renewable 70
   renewable 70

environment 28

enzyme 12, 14

evaporation 32, 33, 35

excretion 9

expansion 39

eye 7

faeces 12

fat 11

fertilisation 17, 19, 21

fibre 11

filtration 35

flower 21

flowering plant 21

foetus 17

food 11

food chain 29

food web 29

force 57, 60
   balanced 57
   turning 59
   unbalanced 58

formula 34

freezing 32

frequency 65

friction 56, 58, 60

fruit 21, 22

fuel 9
   fossil 70

function 7

fungi 25

gamete 19, 22

gas 32

genetic information 22

germination 22

glucose 14, 20

gravitational attraction 67

groups 24

growth 9

habitat 28

health 18

hearing 65

herbivore 29, 30

hertz (Hz) 65

hormone 16, 19

immunisation 18

indicator 50

inheritance 26

insulator 53, 56

invertebrate 26

joint 12, 13

joule (J) 72

kidney 7

leaf 7

life processes 7, 9

ligament 12, 13

light 62

liquid 32

living things 7
   groups of 25
   kingdoms of 25

loudness 65

luminous 62, 66, 69

lung 13

magnet 54, 55

magnetic field 54, 55

magnetism 54

medicine 18

melting 32, 33, 38

melting temperature 38

menstrual cycle 17

menstruation 17

metals 43, 46

microbe 18

mineral 11

mirror 63

mixture 34

model 32, 37

molecule 33

moment 59, 60
   anticlockwise 59
   clockwise 59

moon 68

motion 57

movement 9

muscle 12, 13
   antagonistic pair 13

neutral 50

neutralisation 51, 52

neutron 33

newton (N) 59

newton metre 59

nicotine 18

night-time 68

non-luminous 62, 66, 69

non-metal 46

normal line 63

nucleus 8, 9
nutrition 9

offspring 24
omnivore 29, 30
orbit 67
organ 7
    system 14
organism 7
ossicle 65, 66
ovary 16, 17
ovulation 16
oxygen 13, 14, 20

parent 24
particle 32
    model 32
pathogen 18
penis 16, 17
periodic table 36
petal 21
pH 50, 52
photosynthesis 20
physical change 38
pitch 65
pivot 59
placenta 17
planet 67
plant kingdom 25
poison 30
pole 55
pollen 21
    tube 21
pollination 21
pollutant 44
pollution 44
population 29
predator 29, 30

pregnancy 17
pressure 59, 60
prey 30
producer 29, 30
product 42, 44
protein 11
proton 33
puberty 16
pyramid of numbers 29

reactant 44
reactions 42–48
    combustion 42
    decomposition 43
    displacement 43
    neutralisation 43, 51
    oxidation 42
    reduction 43
    with metals 47
reactivity series 47
reflection 62, 63
refraction 63, 64
relay 55
reproduction 9, 16, 21
reproductive system 16
repulsion 53, 55, 56
resistance, electrical 54
respiration 9, 13, 14
    aerobic 14
respiratory system 13
rock 40
    cycle 40
    igneous 40
    metamorphic 40
    sedimentary 40
root hair 8, 20

salt 52

satellite 68
    artificial 68
    natural 68
scattering 62, 66
season 68
seed 21
    dispersal 22
selective breeding 25
sensitivity 9
sepal 21
sexual intercourse 17
shadow 62
skeleton 12
smoking 18
Solar System 67
solid 32
solubility 39
solute 39
solution 39
    saturated 39
solvent 39
sound 62
space 62
species 24, 26
spectrum 64, 66
speed 57, 60
stamen 21
star 67
stigma 21
style 21
Sun 67, 70
switch 54

temperature 71
tendon 12, 13
testis 16, 19
thermal energy 33, 71
tissue 14

trachea 13
transducer 71

umbilical cord 17
universal indicator 50
urethra 17
uterus 16, 17

vaccine 18
vacuole 8
vacuum 62, 66
vagina 17
variation 24, 26
    environmental causes 24
    inherited causes 24
vertebrate 26
vibration 32, 65
virus 18
vitamin 11
voltage 54

water 11, 39
wave 64
wavelength 65
weathering 39, 41
word equation 42

year 69